STRANGERS TO THIS GROUND

Cultural Diversity in Contemporary American Writing

W. M. FROHOCK

SOUTHERN METHODIST UNIVERSITY PRESS
DALLAS

810.9
F

For Jacques Voisine
and
René Fréchet

en souvenir du train de huit heures

Foreword

THIS BOOK had its beginning in weekly conversations with the Frenchmen to whom it is dedicated. Every Wednesday morning from February to June in 1958 we took the train together from Paris to Lille, where we were lecturing at the university. My companions knew English perfectly and were familiar with the American landscape, having perhaps traveled about the United States more than I, and they were at once so well-read and so open-minded that their hesitations about the quality of American life, and their occasional rejection of what we consider its values, seemed to me to be significant and to call for careful statement of the opposite positions.

From personal observation they were persuaded that the United States lacks cultural variety. They had ridden our cross-country buses, apparently reading David Riesman and William Whyte whenever they tired of looking out of windows or of listening to their other-directed fellow-passengers. What they saw and heard confirmed what they read: America was monotonously like itself, just as Americans were monotonously like each other.

My general answer was, and is, that beneath the superficial uniformity there is variety in abundance. American writing has testified constantly, for fifty years and more, to the fact that the decisive experience in the lives of most Americans is one of adjustment following a move from one cultural area to another. This experience has so often been the subject of what we write that it has exerted a shaping force on our entire literature. If our criticism has not had more to say about it, the reason is that the subject is so continually before our eyes that we frequently lose sight of it. And in addition, much American writing which does not exploit the subject explicitly presupposes it.

By late April the seeming paradox—variety amid monotony—became the burden of a lecture delivered for the USIS at the American Cultural Center in Paris; its substance is the first chapter of this volume. A week later what is now the chapter on Ezra Pound was developed in lectures, given in French, at the Instituts Français of London and Edinburgh. Arguments about other writers, now distributed here and there through the book, were proposed in the weeks following to two audiences at the University of Algiers and one at the Major Seminary of Saint Yves at Saint Brieuc. The material on Scott Fitzgerald and James Gould Cozzens, in briefer form, was presented to the USIS Seminar at Nice in July. Meanwhile my students at the University of Lille had listened tolerantly to what has since become the stuff of chapters on Emily Dickinson and Edna St. Vincent Millay.

With the traces of missionary zeal which such occasions naturally generate now removed, the case for cultural variety still seems reasonably solid. I did not then, and do not now, claim that our diversity is not on the way out: there may well be enormous forces at work to whip the internals of our life into visible conformity just as other enormous ones, principally economic, have whipped the externals. But there is impressive evidence in our literature that the process has still a long way to go.

Accordingly I am bewildered by the frequency with which I find myself in disagreement with David Riesman. *The Lonely Crowd* remains a master work of its decade, but our literature simply does not seem to me to bear out its central thesis regarding the radical change which Riesman sees taking place in the American character. It might, of course, be argued in reply that, since the American writer is a modern artist and since the modern artist is by definition alienated from his society, his testimony is irrelevant and to be discounted. This I doubt, however: our writers as a group may seem to be vestigial remnants of the inner-directed past, but each of them has been read by a very large and sympathetic audience. Arithmetic suggests that if the number of the audience is added to the number of the writers, the resultant total makes the use of such words as *vestige* and *alienation* subject to considerable caution, and commends working in shades of gray as preferable to black and white.

Meanwhile my debt to David Riesman is no smaller than that of anyone who has tried to understand the American past *and* the American present. I am deeply grateful also to my French colleagues with whom this discussion started —and whose views have not been presented here with even the suggestion of the depth and subtlety and completeness of documentation which was characteristic of them. Certain Americans, including especially Arthur Mizener and Harry Levin, may recognize in these pages even more of their ideas than I am aware of—and it would be arrantly ungrateful not to add that among those with whom I have been at pains to underline my disagreement are some, like Lionel Trilling, from whom I have learned much.

It is pleasant to acknowledge here the kindness of the editors of the *Southwest Review* for permission to reprint the chapter on "The Dilemmas of Criticism" and parts of articles on Trilling, Fitzgerald, and Pound which have been incorporated in the present text. Thanks also are due the following for permission to quote:

Charles Scribner's Sons, Inc., for permission to quote from *The Great Gatsby*, by F. Scott Fitzgerald, copyright 1925 by Charles Scribner's Sons and renewal copyright 1953 by Frances Scott Fitzgerald Lanahan; from *Tender Is the Night*, by F. Scott Fitzgerald, copyright 1934 by Charles Scribner's Sons; and from *Across the River and Into the Trees*, by Ernest Hemingway, copyright 1950 by Ernest Hemingway.

The Grove Press, Inc., for permission to quote from *The Subterraneans*, by Jack Kerouac, copyright 1958 by Jack Kerouac.

Harvard University for permission to quote from the *Harvard Gazette*.

Norma Millay Ellis for permission to quote from *Collected Poems*, by Edna St. Vincent Millay, copyrights 1917-1950 by Edna St. Vincent Millay, and 1945-1956 by Norma Millay Ellis.

The Liveright Publishing Corporation, for permission to quote from *A Treasury of Humorous Verse*, by Samuel Hoffenstein, Black & Gold Library, Liveright, Publishers, N.Y. Copyright © 1946, Liveright Publishing Corp.

The Viking Press, Inc., for permission to quote from *The Liberal Imagination*, by Lionel Trilling, copyright 1950 by Lionel Trilling; from *The Opposing Self*, by Lionel Trilling, copyright 1955 by Lionel Trilling; and from *The Dharma Bums*, by Jack Kerouac, copyright 1958 by Jack Kerouac.

To Ruth E. Werman and to Natalie B. Frohock, my wife, for help with the manuscript and for making the index, I offer especially affectionate gratitude.

W.M.F.

Cambridge, Massachusetts
September 12, 1961

Contents

STRANGERS TO THIS GROUND

1

The Great Topos

RIGHT at the end of *The Great Gatsby* there occurs a passage which everyone reads and nobody says much about. Gatsby is dead; the big house at West Egg has been closed and there will be no more parties; Nick Carraway has moved back into New York and found life rather difficult to live. Fitzgerald might have done well to close his novel right here, the story being over and there being little more for Nick to add to his account of his own feelings. But the page goes on:

I see now that this has been a story of the West, after all—Tom and Gatsby, Daisy and Jordan and I, were all Westerners, and perhaps we possessed some deficiency in common which made us subtly unadaptable to Eastern life.

Even when the East excited me most, even when I was most keenly aware of its superiority to the bored, sprawling, swollen towns beyond the Ohio, with their interminable inquisitions which spared only the children and the very old—even then it had always for me a quality of distortion. West Egg, especially, still figures in my more fantastic dreams. I see it as a night scene by El Greco: a hundred houses, at once conventional and grotesque, crouching under a sullen, overhanging sky and a lustreless moon. In the foreground four solemn men in dress suits are walking along the sidewalk with a stretcher on which lies a drunken woman in a white evening dress. Her hand, which dangles over the side, sparkles cold with jewels. Gravely the men turn in at a house—the wrong house. But no one knows the woman's name, and no one cares.

Throughout the story Nick has been noteworthily ambivalent toward Gatsby, alternately repelled and fascinated, sympathetic one moment and disapproving the next. Now he has been disturbed and hurt, and is ambivalent no longer. Gatsby's humiliation has humiliated him. So he will go back home where such misfortunes do not happen, away from a place where people are apparently born to be heels. Life has gone wrong because he and Gatsby and Daisy and Tom have wandered away from the safety of home.

Presumably critics rarely complain about this passage for the good reason that they see nothing wrong with it. It has not seemed worth while for them to raise the question, What under heaven has the fact of the characters being from another part of the country to do with anything that happens to them in the story? Any slum of any big eastern city could have turned out a Gatsby, just as any Merion County or Westport could have produced Tom, Daisy, and Nick. The "Dream" which so dazzled and misled Gatsby certainly pervades places less remote than Minnesota and the Upper Peninsula. And Gatsby could have lived out the same kind of destiny, perhaps more profitably for his business, in one of the voluptuous villages along the shore north of Chicago. The story could have been just the same and Gatsby, afloat in his own swimming pool, would have been just as dead. All that can be said for Nick's ultimate analysis is that it constitutes a mistaken interpretation of the pertinent data. Certainly no necessity for the passage is generated by the story itself, and it shows about Nick Carraway only what he has already revealed very adequately, viz. that he is not a very shrewd analyst of human situations. Yet there the passage is, and we accept it without being disturbed by matter or manner—by intrusive theme or bathos of tone.

But it is less true that we accept than that we just don't notice. Words and tune are so thoroughly familiar that we read with only a part of our attention, just as, without realizing what we are about, we begin humming when we hear a well-known song. Everybody knows that home is the place there is no other place like, that you do leave it even so, that by leaving it you put yourself among strangers, and that from this change come certain discomfort and probable misfortune. This is the theme everyone orchestrates, the almost obligatory subject, the Great American Topos.

In its most obvious manifestation, Thomas Wolfe's mighty voice leads the chorus. His hero leaves home for the state university. From there he goes up to New England, moves back to New York, chases over to England and the Continent, retreats again to New York, and then returns to the home which, when he gets there, has no door to take him in. The lost and by the wind grieved ghost detests the arid, narrow Boston Irish and the gray-faced swarming hordes of New York Jews; in England and on the mainland of Europe (with the possible exception of Germany) he is again an outsider and lost; and when at last he is back in Old Catawba he finds that there also he is a stranger. This is not the whole of the story of Wolfe's heroes, of course; but without this their stories would be nothing. Fitzgerald, beyond doubt, is the more adept novelist. (Eliot was right in calling *The Great Gatsby* the first great advance in fiction since Henry James.) But Wolfe's ghost has one advantage over Fitzgerald's poor lethal little rich boy in knowing that the hope of becoming an insider is bound to be vain, and one advantage over Nick Carraway in recognizing that there is no particular use in going home.

This is not a mere matter of bewilderment resulting from a move from hinterland to metropolis. The same fundamental discomfort can come from moving from one city to another, or from city to smaller town. James T. Farrell's heroes grow up in the cultural enclave of the Irish South Side; the first

great wrench for Danny O'Neill is to move from one part of
Chicago, which is home, to another which is not. It is there
that he really becomes a stranger and afraid. Farrell is more
reticent and also less well supplied with words than Wolfe,
but the essential complaint is the same: when you want to
come home from a hostile world, the return is impossible.
The change in Farrell's books has been only between two
urban environments. Dreiser's Clyde Griffiths moves from
Kansas City to work out his American tragedy in a smaller
town in upstate New York. Lionel Trilling's John Laskell,
who seems rarely to have left the Five Boroughs before,
comes to grief in central Connecticut. Carol Kennicott takes
her Twin City attitudes and dispositions only a short distance, as distances go in America, for them to be crushed in
Gopher Prairie. All the anguish in James Agee's *A Death in
the Family* comes from a marriage of a town-raised girl to
a man who grew up only a few miles away, by Model-T, but
in the hills.

It is not true that the Great Topos remained viable only
for a brief interval, although it is true that Fitzgerald's,
Wolfe's, and Farrell's work—at least the part of it which is
of interest here—fell in the same decade. But Agee's novel
was still in the writing when he died in 1955; Ralph Ellison's
Invisible Man was printed in 1953; Trilling's *The Middle of
the Journey* dates from 1947; and Robert Penn Warren's
work, in which the vein is several times exploited, spreads
over a very long period indeed. What seems nearer the truth
is that over the years the special lyric tone (best example:
Wolfe) has gone out of style. The later books lack the cry
and moan of the wounded personal sensibility. In compensa-
tion, they reveal—often if not always—a greater exertion of
technique and the presupposition that lostness is part of
man's collective fate. But the technique exploits the same
essential situation of an American who, having crossed the

gulf from one culture to another, finds himself unhappy and bewildered.

Ellison is particularly interesting in this respect, because his hero is a Negro and goes through the customary gambit of reactions to a culture conflict to which one is not accustomed. Ellison's hero quits a Negro social situation in Oklahoma to move to another Negro social situation in Harlem. Meanwhile, Ellison being one of those writers who read very widely, the book gives back some characteristically European overtones. It sounds, especially toward the end, like the work of Louis-Ferdinand Céline. Like Bardamu, the protagonist in *Journey to the End of the Night,* his hero is a chronic fugitive; he is running away from Oklahoma, where life has become impossible through no special fault of his own, and goes on running after he hits New York, without ever being able to find a situation such that on a moment's notice he won't have to start running once more. Like Bardamu also, he is running from the hostility of life itself; experience bombards him with so many more meaningless fragments than he can cope with that at the end he is very near insanity; the running develops into a wild, phantasmagorical chase and ends with the hero scuttling down into a coal cellar where he can be safe because invisible. He could be running hand in hand with Céline's eternal victim—but the experience he is running from is our characteristic American one.

Warren, also, stands somewhat apart because of his device of making the clash of cultures itself furnish the elements of a special technique for emphasizing moral implications. His propensity for parallel plots—the story of Private Porsum alongside that of "Bullseye Jerry" Calhoun; of Cass Mastern beside that of the narrator in *All the King's Men;* of the returned buffalo hunter in *Night Rider*—leads to the creation of an irony which guides the ethical judgment of the reader. Warren's culture clashes are indigenous to the land he writes about; men come down from the rocky ridges, or in from the infertile back parishes, to the rich bottom land, and are strangers as much as Wolfe's Eugene Gant is on his first visit to New York. The narrating character, serving as the "central moral consciousness," may be as much in the dark as to whether Willie Stark has been a great man as ever Fitzgerald's Carraway is about the rights and wrongs of Jay Gatsby; the author keeps the moral reins in his own hand by letting a story about a man who remains on one side of the culture gap constitute an implicit commentary on the man who crosses it.

Adding these cases to Agee's and their technical intricacy to his—which was an intricacy so great that his editor admits never knowing where to insert certain passages of the manuscript that were probably intended to constitute some sort of commentary on the rest—one feels urged toward the conclusion that the topos, rather than dying out, has called for increasingly sophisticated efforts of elaboration.

In other words, here are a group of American novelists who, over at least thirty years, have been embroidering the same essential pattern: the American who leaves his home, as he must leave it, soon finds himself in an unpleasant fix. The topos is not the exclusive property of writers of any particular origin; several of these novelists, by family line, are white Anglo-Saxon Protestants, but also in the group are sons of the Irish immigration, a Jew, a Negro, and a second-generation German; and they come from East, South, Middle West. I do not believe that they invented the pattern. The experience of the heroes of Henry James, going off to Europe to find out how it really feels to be an American, and finding out that being one means being seriously ill at ease, is unlike theirs only in that James's people travel farther. Similar, although not centrally important to the story of *Huckleberry Finn,* is the experience of Huck and Jim when, rounding a bend in the river, they come upon the foreign culture, at first ludicrous and then just horrible, of the Grangerfords. If anyone were to suggest, even, that the archetype is Amasa Delano standing in the presence of the inscrutable and dark foreigner I should not object, except to the pushing of the whole idea a bit too boldly. Meanwhile, it is undeniable that among the novelists who have treated this topos in more recent years stand a number who, after Hemingway and Faulkner, rank high. To sum up their testimony, the image of the American hero of our time is the image of a D.P.

A Displaced Person, technically, is an individual with no passport and no identity papers, no place he can return to, no place where he can reasonably be expected to go. If reports on the mental condition of actual political D.P.'s are correct, he is in danger of losing some of his awareness of his own identity. He is not, in any event, supposed to be particularly happy. He is the true "outsider."

Here we come head on into the fact that the two most popular interpretations at present on the market of what it is like to live in the United States are inordinately hard to reconcile. Our best fiction sounds as if the national culture were really an agglomerate of smaller cultures which are different enough from each other to make the ultimate condition of a man who moves from one of them to another a state of bewilderment and confusion. We are, that is to say, hampered by our cultural variety. But if we take the word of our social sciences, we must for some time have been in the grip of forces which have swept us already a long way to such conformity that we may look forward—if forward is the word—to the day when instead of being culturally various we shall constitute one culturally unvaried matrix.

If what we have been reading lately is right, life in the United States today is merely dangerous, and the danger is one we share with everyone else in the world; tomorrow it will be both dangerous and deadly dull, and this prospect is one which, apparently, we face alone. Such, at least, is the impression one gains from his reading of a decade when thought has been dominated by the revelations of scientists: the physicists, through no fault of theirs, have put us in a way either to blow ourselves off the planet with one loud bang or to radiate ourselves off it, gradually, through interference with biological processes; their comrades in economics, sociology, anthropology, and kindred fields have convinced us that the disaster would not make such a towering difference.

There will shortly be many more of us, and the chances are reported to be that we shall be increasingly alike. Everything conspires to turn us more and more into organization men, living lives which are forced upon us by our being what we are, and which in turn make us more completely more of the same. Our society can hardly avoid being affluent, even if it tries its stupid best. Everyone can afford prestige symbols, and can hide embarrassing political, ideological, ethnic, and religious differences under a film of uniformity. Who can tell a Democratic candidate from a Republican? There may be moments each week end, perhaps, when an alert observer can distinguish us as Protestants, Catholics, and Jews; as for distinguishing between varieties of Protestant or Jew, the possibility is glimmering already. We want status, but status of a sort that is available to everybody.

All this may be merely a bad dream after too constant a diet of David Riesman, John K. Galbraith, William Whyte, Will Herberg, Vance Packard, C. Wright Mills, and their myriad colleagues. One would hope so. For the horrid little thought will not down that the termite, for all his admirable social qualities, is an Organization Bug. Galbraith offers solutions to a number of pressing questions, but he has not yet told us what to do after we have televisions in every room; making them stereoscopic will be only a temporary palliative. Riesman has not said why, if the trend toward "other direction" gets out of hand, social intercourse could not conveniently come to consist of talking to the mirror and then playing back the words from a tape-recorder. And if religion, with its embarrassing way of emphasizing differences, eventually becomes intolerable, can't it be replaced by occasional meetings where we can all meditate—no need to talk—upon the Values we hold in common? To President Conant's recent objection, that parochial schools are divisive and therefore bad, an answer is already suggested in Peter De Vries' *The Mackerel Plaza:* in that five-ring Social Center which promises to become the church of the future the community-minded thing to do is manifestly to extirpate the "Worship Area."

The thing to fear about the social scientists is not that they may be leading us up the garden path. The grisly horror is that they may not be. They have us pretty well convinced that the typical American, if he existed, would no longer look like Tocqueville's New Man or Max Weber's resolute practicer of the Protestant Ethic; it is all too evident that our society has changed in cadence with our economy, and the fact comes home with a jolt as soon as we remember that "our society" is here nothing more than a pronoun synonymous with "we." Our basic function is no longer production but consumption; we are socially valuable in proportion to our ability to use up what we make. (Just the other day, when Detroit slumped, it was unpatriotic not to buy a new automobile and keep the tires of the economy wearing away toward Planned Obsolescence.) Any man's bankbook will tell him that fortune does not accrue from the increased creation of goods. Adjusting to the fact, he no longer seeks fortune but security, just as he no longer seeks his own esteem through the attainment of private goals but wants the approval of his peers. We try to be what we think other people want us to be, and they return the compliment; everybody wants to be like everybody else. Working for yourself is no longer preferable to working for a foundation, a corporation, or the government. It is best to be a cog.

An effective cog is distinguished by no individual characteristics, so it gets along well among other cogs. But its cultural potential is low. How do cogs keep awake? And does it make any difference to them if they do?

Enlightened visitors suspect us not only of having destroyed our cultural variety but also of making a virtue of necessity: we live, they say, by a loose ethic of conformity. What else, they want to know, is "The American Way" but a glorification of the principle that it is good to do what everybody does? One recent French visitor accuses us, in a book* which is no less sharp for being outrageously biased, of sending out missionaries, under the cloak of Fulbright, to convert the European world.

Not all these visitors arrive with the disposition of American congressmen on tour and of European intellectuals generally, i.e. with their conclusions formulated before the jet touches down at Idlewild ("Wonderful, your going to England," said Hippolyte Taine to his nephew Chevrillon. "What ideas are you going to verify?"), ready for the quick visits to New York, Cleveland, Kansas City, and Hollywood which persuade them that American hotels are all alike, that bellboys conform everywhere to the same picaresque type, and that mashed potatoes drown easily in gravy. Well-equipped as to language and experienced in being away from home, after adequately long periods in the United States, they report a dispiriting cultural uniformity. They deserve a respectful hearing.

*Cyrille Arnavon, *L'Américanisme et Nous* (Paris, 1958).

Doubtless they overdo the case. Their experience is principally of the superhighway culture. They drive from one coast to the other in cars that look alike, over broad and beautifully engineered but remarkably unvaried highways, buy gasoline at pumps of the same color, eat the same hot dogs, hear the standard-English voices of the radios pouring out the same news, the same baseball scores. The wheat of Kansas waves in the same wind as the wheat of Nebraska and Colorado. Human beings dress, look, talk like each other under the hot American sun. A motel is . . . a motel. And it might be asking a lot to tell them to go a few miles off the highway to see the difference, especially since—as we are all convinced—the difference is one of degree.

Overstate as much as they will, either what such Europeans see now is what we shall all see sooner or later, or else what the social scientists have been telling us has been terribly wrong. Tocqueville was already aware of what could and probably would happen, and whatever else one says about the late Irving Babbitt, the solid part of his criticism was based upon the same fundamental concern. In essence, the social scientists are telling us that something long expected is now upon us.

Yet our literature contradicts the social scientists' view, insistently affirming that cultural diversity is characteristic of America. Our typical experience, the one we have all had at one time or another and which has done so much to make us what we are, is the experience of our own mobility. Motion pervades even our folklore: our heroes have always wanted elbow-room. Large families and small means have meant that for generations the fledglings have been pushed early from the nest—if indeed they have waited to be pushed. Some parts of the country have always been richer than others in jobs. Our idea of education involves displacement:

our idiom makes a special verb of going-away to school. Colleges and universities take for granted that they should be "national," which means that they are eager to get clientele from the largest possible fraction of the fifty states. And in this respect compulsory military service supplements education, because it is good for you to live with people your age who come from "all over." Whoever you are, the chances are that before you are very old you will be living away from home.

Also, the age when one becomes mobile coincides with the age when one begins to write. Consequently we recognize sub-genres in our fiction: the novel of life in the army, the novel of student life—*The Plastic Age, This Side of Paradise, Through the Wheat, The Naked and the Dead, From Here to Eternity.* Sometimes these mention study or combat, as the case may be, but the essential subject of most is a new kind of life among a new kind of people. Both create a kind of indigenous unanimism, in that they bring types together into a group; a Jew from Brooklyn, a taciturn Texan, a Cracker, an Italian from San Francisco, a boy from a New England Saint Grottlesex join in a squad, a ship's company, a fraternity, the entry of a dormitory. A novelist writes about what he knows, and who in America, when he begins to write, knows much else than school or service? At least, this is what they know best, and the novels reveal the fact. What happened to Norman Mailer after *The Naked and the Dead,* to James Jones after *From Here to Eternity?*

Thus the story is so very often one of adjustment: Jews learning to live among Gentiles, Catholics among Protestants, children of Fundamentalists among the children of Liberals, each discovering what he is by seeing himself contrasted with the others, undergoing the first great shock of discovery. The by-product has been a kind of anxiety which is also specifically American.

Europeans, in recent years, have written their share about anxiety and estrangement, telephone lines which do not bring down a voice from the Castle, men who when they hear their voice recorded on the phonograph do not recognize it, characters who draw you aside to tell you about their feelings of guilt and exclusion. But a distinction is in order. The Europeans treat the condition as characteristic of humanity; to be human at all is to live isolated, out of complete communication and condemned to the nameless discomfort which results. The American takes a less cosmic view; his alienation inheres in his being a product of a special kind of civilization—which the European accuses him of wanting to spread over the entire planet. Sixty years ago, when French writers like Barrès created the topos they called deracination, the heroes did not have to cope with an anxiety born of their leaving the provinces to live in Paris; they merely lost their moral bearings there and got themselves into trouble. In this, doubtless, they were nearer the condition of our Americans than are the people of Camus, Malraux, and Kafka, in that the difficulty was local and practical, physically factual more than metaphysical. The American is a D.P. within a definite setting which he tends to take with him even when he leaves America. By this I mean, for example, that in World War II, when several million Americans had their first experience of living outside the United States, their contact with the foreign life was minimal; their camps were pieces of the United States and they regarded the rest of the countries they were in as immense native compounds, the inhabitants of which were considered to be "Gooks." (The ECA colony in Paris in 1950 still dedicated great effort to finding restaurants where you could get a steak like in Kansas City.) Even Ernest Hemingway's nomads, for all their extensive savvy regarding the native population, sound like experienced missionaries who have acquired a practical,

working knowledge of rather complex heathen. Our displacement, like our speech, is characteristically our own.

But why, then, are we so unaware of how thoroughly
we justify the reservation David Riesman makes with respect
to his own thesis, to the effect that no culture is all of a piece,
and of the special nature of what might even be called the
American Predicament? A partial answer, at least, may lie
in the political stalemate into which we have fallen since
the end of World War II. We are, to be blunt about it, afraid.
It is not merely that we are embarrassed by finding ourselves
saddled with international responsibilities for which we have
to educate ourselves as we go; we are also aware, for the
first time in our history, of having been jockeyed into a position where we cannot be sure of coming out on top. Somebody very different from us sits across the globe looking
rather unpleasant. And our natural reaction is to huddle
together, to disguise our differences from ourselves, to take
comfort in a superficial unity. Anything that makes us feel
welded together appeals; anything that can be thought divisive is bad. It may be symptomatic here that when President
Conant condemned secondary education under religious
auspices as divisive, he felt no need at all to explain why
division is necessarily bad. Possibly an even more remarkable
symptom is that when proponents of religiously sponsored
schools replied to him they took the line that what they
advocated was not "really" so divisive as it looked. Nobody
argued that a nation which has from the start lived in division
on any number of crucial issues should be strong enough to
go on doing so. One could assume that we were afraid of our
own cultural diversity. Perhaps we are.

Meanwhile we ought perhaps to be more afraid still of
the various consequences of misunderstanding ourselves.
Obviously, our writers of these last decades, from the Lost
Generation to the Beats, have been more affected by the

diversity of our cultures than by any danger of our becoming an undifferentiated cultural lump. Thus they have returned, in different moods and tones, to the Great Topos, testifying thereby that to certain Americans at least—perhaps not representative ones, perhaps unrepresentatively alienated but important even so because their testimony is important writing—either the illusion or the reality of cultural diversity has existed and still to some extent exists. To read them, one would sometimes feel justified, even, in talking not about an American culture but about a plurality of cultures within the Commonwealth.

If the situation is not completely comfortable, and leaves us feeling helpless to do anything to ward off the workings of those mysterious forces of which we laymen know little more than that they are apparently beyond our control, even so there is still some benefit to be got from it: at least it can make us see, a little better than we have in the past, the meaning of some of our literature.

Only in the process of rereading the criticism which has piled up over the years on the subject of these "alienated," lost, homeless writers does one realize how often they are taxed with the same defect—a certain failure to continue growing up and to produce, as they grow older, works of increasingly mature tone and of greater wisdom. By and large, the criticism is right: our literary history is too often a tale of unkept promise. This is almost as much a topos of our criticism as the Great Topos is of our imaginative literature. It would be possible to find support for the allegation of a causal connection between the two: the experience of social or cultural adjustment tends to stop, or radically to slow down, the ripening process.

We do not know that any such thing is true in any absolute sense. Logically there is no reason why the experience of moving from culture to culture should not produce a rapidly maturing, wise individual. But the fact is that certain writers, like their young heroes, have not been subject to this logic. And there is, furthermore, a disquieting tendency on the part of current criticism to *assume,* in the face of contrary evidence, that writers do not mature. Thomas Wolfe was a wiser man by the time he wrote *You Can't Go Home Again,* but the novel which is regularly taken to represent his work is *Look Homeward, Angel;* similarly, Scott Fitzgerald will always be the author of *The Great Gatsby,* and the evidence of *The Last Tycoon* will continue to be generally overlooked. Who remembers that a long time after she had stopped burning her candle at both ends, Edna St. Vincent Millay wrote *Conversation at Midnight?* It is not absolutely necessary to cross a culture gap in order to stay unripened: see the case of Emily Dickinson, who, whatever else may have happened to her, moved about so little that it must have happened right in Amherst, Massachusetts. Conversely, crossing one does not inevitably arrest development: see Henry James.

Thus no broad generalization is in order, but on the other hand it is not out of order to study the possible effects of such a typical experience upon a collection of typical Americans.

2

Lionel Trilling and the American Reality

COOL and remote—as if he were rather detached from both his subject and his reader—Lionel Trilling's prose runs as if he were talking to someone he respects but does not know very well, about something which interests him without stirring his enthusiasm very much. His introduction to Orwell's *Homage to Catalonia* furnishes a characteristic example:

It was an odd statement for a young man to make nowadays, and I suppose that what we found so interesting about it was just this oddity—its point was in its being an old-fashioned thing to say. It was archaic in its bold commitment of sentiment, and it used an archaic word in an archaic simplicity. Our pleasure was not merely literary, not just a response to the remark's being so appropriate to Orwell, in whom there was indeed a quality of an earlier day. We were glad to be able to say it about anybody. One doesn't have the opportunity very often.

He assumes a general agreement between himself and his audience about such subjects as politics, morals, and taste. "We of the liberal persuasion...," he begins a sentence somewhere, and it is clear that he is addressing a reader already trained and broken in to a way of seeing life, who has possibly sat at Trilling's feet at Columbia once upon a time, and who is one of the happy few. From this band of brothers the tone of Trilling's prose probably leaves no few other readers feeling somewhat excluded. The disadvantage of the style is self-evident; the corresponding advantage is that for those who can take it a maximum of communication and a minimum of lost and strayed meaning are guaranteed.

Those who take it most avidly belong to the group who grew up on the *New Freeman,* the *New Republic,* and the *Nation,* and who now subscribe to the *Partisan Review*—but read *Kenyon* and *Sewanee* now and then in the public library. The term Intellectual is honorific in their ears even if in modesty they refuse to attach it to themselves. They are earnestly interested in ideas, especially new ones. Wherever they live, their spiritual home is New York. They have confidence in Trilling and in return he, obviously, has confidence in them.

I suspect this confidence that he will be understood underlies and makes possible his unique achievement. Like most of our practicing critics, Trilling is a college professor— and this means not a writer kept by an institution to sweeten the campus atmosphere but a genuine and more or less willing victim of academic routine. Yet unlike a worrisome number whose names have become familiar in the years which have seen criticism become a respected discipline in the Academy, he manages not to sound like a professor when he writes. Better still, he does not sound like a professor trying not to sound like a professor. The trouble with most of us pedants being that we sound exactly like what we are, Trilling has very little company indeed. The tone of his criticism is distinctive and instantly recognizable. He hardly needs to sign his work.

The pity is that, being a professor and thus busy, he has not written as much as one could wish. His *Matthew Arnold* was originally his Doctor's thesis; *E. M. Forster* is a too brief introduction to the works of the novelist; the little book on Freud appears to be the extension of something originally conceived as an article. Apart from these, his criticism is available only through his occasional articles and reviews, not all of which have been collected in *The Liberal Imagination* (1950), *The Opposing Self* (1955), and *A Gathering of Fugitives* (1956). Trilling's own tendency to discount the unity of his work, to insist that what he writes is only what someone invites him to write, has the effect of heightening— in some quarters at least—the impression that he publishes only his *disjecta membra*; and it is perfectly true that *The Opposing Self* contains mostly his introductions to reprints which one publisher or another put him to doing, and *A Gathering of Fugitives* brings together critical essays he wrote for the house periodical of a select little book club. If we took at face value the lack of pound for pound bulk and his own disclaimer, it would be very hard to see how what he has done could be sufficient to justify the reputation he enjoys.

The truth is, I think, that the unity of Trilling's work, if one knows where to look for it, is far more imposing than he wants to admit. It does not lie in the subjects he has dealt with. I would prefer to call it, rather, a unity of concern. About the most scattered and disparate subjects he is forever asking the same questions: about the moral implications of our arts, about the ideational substructure of politics, about the position or predicament of an intellectual class in an anti-intellectual world, about the impact of our discoveries of the irrational and subrational, about the relation of fiction to the structure of society, about the nature of culture itself. These questions come up no matter what Trilling is scrutinizing, and to such an extent that sometimes the work he criticizes seems to become only a pretext for the further elaboration of one of his favorite preoccupations. One could make a metaphor about a subterranean ledge (which would be the body of Trilling's thought) mostly buried beneath

the surface but with here, there, and elsewhere a corner of
stone, which would be an article or study, sticking up
through into the light: each corner would look different
enough from the others, but all would be made of the same
essential stuff. Trilling's one novel, *The Middle of the Journey* (1947), treats the same matters he has worried constantly in his critical writing.

Arnold has always been, if not accurately speaking a
model for him, at least an example of the kind of critic he
would like to be. Throughout a period when criticism as an
enterprise in this country has tended to avoid the issues
which preoccupy the rest of the world in favor of a closer
and closer scrutiny of texts, Trilling has constantly maintained that since literature, art, ideas, and social attitudes
are all manifestations of a culture, the subject of ultimate
interest for the critic is the culture itself. It should surprise
no one that one of his best performances was elicited not by
a piece of literature at all but by the so-called "Kinsey
Report." This need not and does not mean that Trilling is
given to sermons inspired by texts like "Wragg is in custody."
In fact, to judge by his recent writing, he is less disposed to
alarmed homiletics than the situation would warrant. He is
more occupied with interpretation and the drawing of fine
but minor discriminations than with passing apocalyptic
judgments. But still, what he interprets and draws his discriminations about is, ultimately, our culture; and in this
sense he is Arnoldian. He even has to accept, as Arnold also
did, occasional imputations of snobbery.

His self-conscious interest in cultural phenomena not only
sets Trilling apart from the body of American critics but also
raises questions about him which in the cases of other American critics hardly arise. Other critics can get away with far
more. The most horrendous failure to catch the point about
Emily Dickinson, for example, does not mean that the ordi-

nary critic who stumbles into error in her case will not prove
entirely adequate when he turns to give an account of Walt
Whitman. So long as the poets are studied as individuals,
one or a dozen slip-ups do not disqualify. But if a critic
approaches each of his subjects as the manifestation of a
culture, anything that goes wrong with his perceptions is
bound to start us wondering about how well he understands
our culture as a whole. The defect, however small, is capable
of extending its influence indefinitely. The commitment to
see life steadily and see it whole involves the assumption of
a very broad responsibility.

At the same time, the nature of Trilling's work places an
obligation upon anyone who thinks that he sees a serious
defect in it to delimit with great care the area which he
believes the fault to affect. The body of cultural materials
with which Trilling deals is by no means specifically American. Much that he writes has to do with nineteenth-century
England, and he has a fair amount to say about what has
been written and thought on the Continent. His political
awareness takes in much which is not indigenously American. And, of course, he has written cogently about Freud. No
small part of his criticism has as much significance on the
other side of the ocean as it does here and he has, as a
matter of fact, an attentive following in England. As an
interpreter of English and continental writings to American
readers he is, all in all, admirable, and our admiration need
not diminish if we also note that his understanding of America is not so completely satisfactory.

I mean that somehow—and possibly only from time to
time—his perspective on the culture of the United States
seems to be curiously foreshortened. This is not, I insist, quite
the same thing as taking up the old refrain that New York
is not America, or coextensive with America. But it is, on
the other hand, saying that from the eminence of Morning-

side Heights certain rather marked aspects of the hinterland
are not particularly visible; certain cultural variations, some
of them quite visible when one is in their neighborhood, tend
to disappear. Everyone knows that they exist. David Riesman
never made a truer remark than the one in *The Lonely
Crowd:* "No culture is all of a piece," nor one with which
there was more general agreement. But certain as we are
of this fact, it is a hard one to keep in mind when the
evidence is not before our eyes.

Trilling's novel, *The Middle of the Journey,* is built
around such an experience of cultural diversity. The hero,
John Laskell, goes to Connecticut to convalesce from a grave
illness, and there finds himself very much out of place. An
inveterate New Yorker, he fails to establish communication
with the locals of Crannock—which can surely be no farther
from New York than Farmington. This alienation leads
to his being partly responsible for a horrid disaster. The
child Susan, whom he watches prepare her "piece" to
speak at the village bazaar, uses the traditional wooden gestures of the rural elocutionist. Laskell tries to teach her
different and more appropriately "natural" ones. The change
throws off the little girl's memory; at the bazaar she forgets
her lines, displeasing her drunken father; he strikes her and
she dies of heart failure.

The girl's death is not really Laskell's fault, for her heart
has always been weak and the father has always been unpre-
dictable; Laskell has merely set off a chain reaction. But it
remains true that the immediate cause of the disaster is his
ignorance: Trilling's hero just doesn't know that the wooden
gestures he has corrected are more appropriate for "speaking
a piece" than are his "natural" but imported ones. His misfortune crowns a series of minor failures; his brief liaison
with the little girl's mother, Emily, is the nearest he has come
to being able to "talk with" the people of the place, and the

only contact in which he has not felt himself a stranger and the object of suspicion.

Admirers of *The Middle of the Journey* will remind me that the novel is not "about" Laskell's estrangement in Connecticut, but about the plight of the intellectuals and their difficulties in adapting themselves as the communist dream recedes. They are right, and precisely because they are right, Trilling's novel is already irremediably dated. Its climate is the climate of the Hiss-Chambers case; there is already a whole generation of readers in the country who need glosses to understand why Laskell's ex-Communist friend Maxim has run away in panic. But my point is that the part of the story which is not dated is the one which deals with Laskell's disorientation in the Connecticut countryside. I would not have thought that it would require glosses of any kind.

But apparently it does require them; at least, something in the novel itself suggests the necessity. Laskell, who by the way is no fool, seems to misunderstand his own situation, or so one is forced to conclude by what seems to be the meaning of an important episode. A wealthy old lady from Boston needs a new maid. She crooks a finger and the local wench who has been with Laskell's hosts, the Crooms, as "hired girl" directly packs up and quits her job. Now there is nothing in the event itself to surprise anyone experienced in American life. What surprises is Laskell's interpretation of what has happened: he sees the incident as the product of a class rivalry. As he sees it, a member of the squirearchy has spoken and the yokel has obeyed.

One thing is very clear: Laskell is certainly *not* in touch with the ways of the place. As anyone could have told him— had he asked—the hired girl's departure is not a function of class at all. The old lady may be as rich as she wants—still what gets the girl to move is not the money but the fact that the old lady is established in the place. She has been here a

long time. On money alone she might indeed have persuaded
the girl to move her job, but the chances are against it. She
and the girl are in a position to understand each other's
ways; in her new place the girl will not be aware of the
culture gap which she cannot help feeling as she works for
Laskell's New Yorker, late-arrival friends.

Now Trilling has the novelist's right not to be responsible
for the behavior of the people in his novels so long as they
behave in character. But that Laskell's behavior *is* in character is part of my point. Also, nothing in the novel suggests
that the author feels Laskell's understanding of the situation
to be anything less than completely right. Since Laskell is
the point-of-view character—and operating in the third
person so that a comment from the author would be easily
possible—one is just a bit perturbed not to find comment
forthcoming. It is surely a curious choice to have placed in
the point-of-view position, in a novel which is "about" the
predicament of the intellectual in America, an intellectual
who can get lost in Crannock, Connecticut.

Laskell's dilemma in *The Middle of the Journey* seems
to me to foreshadow Trilling's difficulty in *The Liberal Imagination.* The "underhum" of manners in which Trilling is so
interested in his criticism seems merely a meaningless buzz-
ing in the ears of the hero of his novel. Lacking a firm class
structure, says Trilling the critic, America lacks a fully developed novel. And somehow, one gathers, only the firmly
class-structured society produces the "underhum" of manners the novel needs. But, like Laskell, he seems to close his
ears to the great source of "underhum"—which approaches
the thunderous—rising from the frictions of our various
cultures.

No one is likely to contest Trilling's reason why the kind
of novel we have in America is not the kind that has flourished in Europe. His touchstones of fiction are, chiefly, the

works of Dostoevski and Tolstoy, of Stendhal and Balzac (perhaps also of Flaubert and Proust) among the continentals, and of the English nineteenth-century novelists. Very often in such novels the archetypal experience is that of a character from one level of society coming somehow into contact with life at another level; the tensions which develop in the individual derive from the tensions existing in the society he moves in. It would be an exaggeration, of course, to say that society was the unique source of such tensions, even in English country-house fiction, and more clearly still in the fiction of the Continent. Julien Sorel and Eugène de Rastignac are taken up, to be sure, with moving from one social class to another. But at the same time they are country boys who have come to the big city; Tolstoy's Levin is torn between life in his province and life in the capital. But, all this being granted, Trilling's view is essentially right. The social material of the great European novels was what he says it was.

Yet perhaps there is more to the story. Almost inevitably the novels he prefers are adventures into the socially unfamiliar, with the story seen either by someone who shares the feeling of unfamiliarity or else by someone to whom the social situation is old hat, who watches some newly arrived individual orient himself: Frédéric Moreau learning his way about in Flaubert's Paris would be representative of one kind, Marcel watching Dr. Cottard in the Verdurins' salon (through the eyes of Swann) would represent the other. Trilling's belief that most novels are stories of an "initiation" recognizes this unfamiliarity as an important element in fiction. I would like to suggest that the essential element, the element that fiction would be hard put to get along without, is exactly this one of unfamiliarity, rather than the presence of a class-structured society.

Of course this view of what makes a novel a novel is not

exclusively Trilling's, and if other critics had used it with
anything like the discretion and discrimination he has shown
I should not, probably, be so eager to poke holes in it here.
But for several decades now this view has had a fortune it
does not entirely deserve. Since the beginning of the James
boom—which, for convenience, I would date from 1934 and
the James number of *Hound and Horn*—the notion that only
one set of social conditions could permit the novel to flourish
has been held as rigid dogma and has blighted much American criticism. It is as if from too exclusive a contemplation
of the case of Henry James—so exclusive that a vast amount
of other fiction moved completely out of focus—came the
conviction that something in the nature of American society
made the writing of real novels impossible. At first glance the
syllogism seems unattackable: only a firmly (but not too
firmly) stratified society can furnish the materials of which
novels are made; the society of the United States is not
firmly stratified; therefore the novel in the United States is
out of the question. And the corollary is that the best we can
hope for is romances.

The beauty of this logic is in the structure of the syllogism, and vanishes when the structure is taken down so that
the terms may be examined. The major hides an undemon-
strated assumption that a firmly stratified society actually
existed somewhere or other at the time when the novels were
written of which the proponents of the theory approve. But
was there ever a society, anywhere, that really fitted the bill,
or is this an illusion bred of distance in time? We have gradually given up the convenient notion, for instance, that there
was, anywhere in Europe, *one* bourgeoisie, unanimous in the
values it honored and in recognizing its own identity. The
professional middle class was never, it appears, impressed
by its identity with the industrialists; the owner of small
private properties hardly saw eye to eye in many matters

with the proprietor of public enterprises. And if this was true, say, in France, one may be permitted a bit of skepticism about the existence of monolithic (if somewhat fluid) social classes in Britain.

It may be significant that this notion had its first moment of fine careless rapture during the Great Depression. A whole generation of critics, many of whom had never before shown that they knew social problems existed, had suddenly been forced to subject the society they lived in to eager if untutored scrutiny. What they saw was nothing to fall in love with: it was disorderly, and disorder was not particularly commendable. One cannot help sympathizing with minds which in the circumstance made a myth of the way men lived together a hundred years before them. Their nostalgia for a neat orderliness is completely understandable, and so is the fact that in a short time they built up the cliché of the novelist's purview being essentially a "Vision of Order." No vision of order, no real novelist. Nobody happened to ask what would be the trouble with a nice clear Vision of Disorder as the basis for a novel. A disciplined unchaotic society generates values which are generally accepted throughout its structure (although how the process works may not be demonstrable with the same clarity), and these values in turn provide the meanings by which human actions are understandable. (I.e., and e.g., if a girl gets illicitly pregnant almost any member of the society, on whatever level he moves, will agree that she has been "bad.") In other words, which are Richard Blackmur's, "The novel is ethics in action." And the novel required consensus as to ethical standards, especially at a time when economic pressures seemed to have obscured such consensus as there had ever been. Of a juncture when such unlikely co-choristers as Ezra Pound and Irving Babbitt were chanting the necessity of Order, with T. S. Eliot and the critics of the novel joining in, some cheap pun might be possible about the order of the day.

Now it would be hard to deny that English country-house novels required the tidy society of which country houses were a part. But the total effect of this line of thinking was a radical reduction in the going definition of the novel form. Probably it is a libel on Mark Schorer to repeat the canard that once, cornered in a public discussion and forced to name the novels that completely satisfied his notion of what the novel should be, he limited the repertory to the works of Jane Austen. I do not believe the yarn, but on the other hand it must be clear that the tendency of his criticism had to be what it was for the joke to get the currency it had.

Actually, no one has ever demonstrated that the novel *has* to be about what happens to people as they move from layer to layer in a society which is organized horizontally. There are a number of very great ones which have heroes who move, in the course of the story, from one culture to another. Balzac's Rastignac, for example, in *Old Goriot,* and a number of young men in *Lost Illusions* come from provincial homes where life still is in all important respects unchanged from what it was before the Revolution. Tolstoy's Levin moves between the somewhat frenchified culture of St. Petersburg and the very primitive one of the peasants with whom he swings a scythe. And in such cases, of course, the story becomes one, not of values common to all concerned, but of a conflict of values. One could argue, even, that a novel like *Madame Bovary* dramatized a clash of values held by differing groups within what we still think of too often as an undifferentiated bourgeoisie. And what about the so-called "initiation to life" novels, most of which take their interest from the effect of a first contact with a culture which is new to the central character? And what about Proust?

What such theories amount to is hardly more than the

allegation that certain novels, mostly English, required a stable and coherent social order—a fact that few have ever doubted. They do not, of themselves, exclude the possibility of the novel in America or explain why America has not produced more great novels. As Riesman remarks, it is characteristic of the American not to "know which way is up," but so far as literature is concerned he does not need to; he knows which way is away—away from life as he is used to living it, toward a life to which he is unaccustomed—and this knowledge can perfectly well suffice as the basis of some important fiction. It has in fact done so.

Probably it is not exactly cricket to keep reverting to what a critic has said in the rapidly receding past without balancing the account with reference to what he has said more recently; but much of Trilling's most interesting criticism was printed before 1950, before he became engaged in the semiprivate communications of a book club, and he has not returned very often to the same subjects since those early days. One has to assume that he would be willing today to sign what he wrote two decades ago, at least so far as the general trend of his ideas is concerned; he has not repudiated them. But in any event I am less interested at this point in chipping away the reputation of a critic whose work I respect than I am in insisting upon the limits which his critical disposition imposes upon him. It seems to me that insistence upon linking the fate of the novel to one kind of social order condemns one to an incomplete and somewhat deformed view of American fiction. And I believe, in particular, that it also obscures the truth about an important moment in the development of an area of the novel about which we still have to make up our minds.

Trilling's pages on Dreiser, in *The Liberal Imagination*, were written in the context of the late F. O. Mathiessen's attempt to show that Dreiser had not been such a bad manip-

ulator of prose as current criticism believed. After ruining—
definitively in my opinion—the contention of people like
E. B. Burgum that Dreiser's writing is authentically collo-
quial, Trilling goes on to show that Dreiser's diction is no
better than his thought, which is muddled, undisciplined,
uneducated, unoriginal, and vulgar. Then he adds, in a footnote on the Dreiser chapter of *The Literary History of the
United States,*

That he [Dreiser] was a child of his class and time is also true,
but this can be said of everyone without exception; the question
for criticism is how he transcended the imposed limitations of
his time and class. As for the defence made on the ground
of his particular class, it can only be said that liberal thought
has come to a strange pass when it assumes that a plebeian
origin is accountable for a writer's faults through all his
intellectual life.

Trilling's remark is justified, of course, by the historian's
defense of Dreiser's style on the argument that it was conditioned by social class, and so far as it goes it is all right. But
it is very doubtful that if the argument is allowed to stay on
the level of class the whole truth about Dreiser's style can
ever out. Of course it is true that to the extent Dreiser can
be said to have belonged to a social class, that class of recent
immigrants was not educated—at least in English—to a point
where disciplined, discriminating thought could be expected
of it; but it has to be added that while few would want to
defend, today, the quality of Dreiser's thinking, defective
thinking is not the only bad thing, and perhaps not the
worst, in his prose. Trilling would probably agree that
Dreiser was also a victim of imprecision in feeling, that he
does not know the nature of an emotion, and so never can
find the word to define it. What we know about how his characters feel is very largely what we infer from what they do.

And, to judge from his more personal writing, he is hardly more capable of saying, with any accuracy, how he feels himself. Even in the passage Trilling has quoted as an example of "fine" writing, I suspect the real difficulty is that Dreiser does not properly know what his own feelings are and is taking refuge from his own vagueness in the inappropriate adjective and the false tone.

But this emotional looseness does not seem to be Dreiser's exclusive specialty. Look, for example, into the style of *Winesburg, Ohio,* and see how many times Sherwood Anderson has to hide his ignorance of his characters behind explanations of their "passionate" intensity, longing, hunger, or whatever it happens to be. And in pieces like his famous open letter to Margaret Anderson (written in lieu of a review of her book about the *Little Review*) see how, instead of defining how he feels, he flops over into the most inexplicit sentimentality. *Winesburg's* dedication to Anderson's mother, "whose keen observations on the life about her first awoke in me the hunger to see below the surface of lives," is revelatory: the operative word is "hunger." The new realism that grew up in the United States in the second decade of the century and flowered in the third had two beliefs. One was that the little, ordinary man had his story, too: *Spoon River, Winesburg,* Lewis' *Babbitt,* etc. The other was that this fact itself is often touching. The fine indignation about social abuses which animates much of European realism is remarkably lacking. In essence, the American attitude toward the mute, inglorious George Willards has most of the undertones familiar in English writing since Thomas Gray. And not in Dreiser, Anderson, and Masters alone; the deficiency persists in Ernest Hemingway, whose great discovery was that in the circumstances the only remedy is to understate, and in Scott Fitzgerald, who made a similar discovery, perhaps, but not soon enough.

Now if anything is clear about these writers it is that while they did not come from the same social background—not to say class, since for a class to exist it has to recognize itself and its members have to identify themselves with it—they did come from the same part of the country. This is not to disparage the Middle West; most of our good writing, for a long time, came from there. It is only natural and right that the prevailing sensibility of the middle western small town should have pervaded such literature in spite of the change in literary modes, expressing itself sometimes in such unexpected ways as, for instance, the great difficulty experienced by Sinclair Lewis in recognizing the element of satire in his own novels, a difficulty revealed in his correspondence with his publisher.

However valuable a criticism of culture based on the concept of social classes may be, such aspects of our literary history as this one are very likely to be closed off from it. Trilling's perception regarding the absence of colloquialism in Dreiser's writing tells us much about Dreiser and the unperceptiveness of some of his other critics, but does not tell us all there is to learn about Dreiser's style. It would be possible, I believe, to demonstrate that what Trilling puts down as uncolloquial actually reveals a conflict between two styles, a genteel, more or less accepted middle western one (see Tarkington) and the other a personal creation, never fully realized, demanded by Dreiser's perspective on his material. This leaves us only one step short of realizing that the characteristic mark of Dreiser's style is a great insecurity and uncertainty of taste which leads him into the blunders by which we know him. It is bound to remain unrecognized so long as we remain unaware of the variations of regional taste and their power over what has been written in America.

Curiously, our literary critics seem to be less observant and aware of this point than our social scientists. The latter, if I understand them, are most successful when they contrive to generalize, broadly and validly, from particular data, whereas critics succeed, by definition, when they account with great specificity for particulars. In the circumstances it is hard to understand how a David Riesman—taking him once more as an example because Trilling clearly respects his work—turns out to be so much more aware of the particulars, of the exceptions to his rules, than is Trilling. How much of the secret of certain American writers is hidden under the particulars of minute culture variation!

This is not to tax Trilling with ignorance. My complaint is rather that, knowing as much as he does, he does not adopt the stance which would let him make full use of all he knows. One can, as he has demonstrated, be an excellent critic of one sort without paying the least attention to culture variations. But a report of American culture which leaves them out cannot be really complete; it will hardly see what he calls "the American reality" steadily and whole. It will be constantly tempted to forget that the moral phenomenon of life in a border state was necessary compromise, and that the final dribbling-off of *Huckleberry Finn* into Tom-Sawyerism was a characteristic border-state compromise. It is likely to dismiss the background of Faulkner's novels, the richest background any novelist has created in the last fifty years, as "provincial." It is likely to forget that Carol Kennicott went to Gopher Prairie not from an eastern seaboard city but from Minneapolis. Yet, from one point of view at least, such things are what the American reality is made of.

3

F. Scott Fitzgerald: Manners and Morals

ONE IS BORN, say, in Minnesota and migrates eventually to the eastern seaboard; and when one becomes a novelist one's perspectives are very largely determined by the experience of having migrated. In one possible case the novels look back from the East toward home; the novelist's name is Sinclair Lewis and he fights forever the battle of Main Street; change the title as often as he will, such will always be the subject of those of his novels which claim a place in the first rank. In another case the novels dwell on the lives of easterners as lived in the East—wherever you find them, this is their life-style—and are never quite able to see them as do other easterners, but always see in some measure at least from the angle of back home; and now the novelist's name is Scott Fitzgerald. Admitting the egregious differences between the two men, they are comparable: more complex and consequently more durably interesting, Fitzgerald is a Lewis turned inside out. And it is in order to ask whether a criticism which is intent upon grasping "the American reality" does not have to raise the question what the inevitable migration—the simple fact of having changed base from one part of the country to another—meant to the work of such writers.

How does this question apply to Fitzgerald? No one contests, of course, the fact that his being a transplant had something to do with his gaining the special perspective which let him see the life around him as if no one had ever seen it before. But someone has to ask, also, whether being a transplant did not limit the perspective and keep him from being even better than he was.

Fitzgerald now seems to us to have been a kind of exoticist who wrote about a bright, brittle kind of life whose attraction, for his audience, lay in its unfamiliarity. A part of him thus functioned as his reader's surrogate. The significance of this becomes clear if one compares his attitude with Hemingway's and *The Great Gatsby* with *The Sun Also Rises.* Jake Barnes tells his story in a tone which assumes that you know already what the central experience is all about. This kind of complicity between author, character, and reader is exactly what Fitzgerald's stance does not let him achieve. In *The Great Gatsby,* in *Tender Is the Night,* and (one gathers from the notes even more than from the published draft) in *The Last Tycoon,* the characters of Nick, Rosemary, and Cecilia Brady are *on* the scene but not completely *of* it; they stay near the edge to help the reader see in, without being completely in themselves. All of them, so to speak, are in some measure transplants from Minnesota.

Fitzgerald felt the need of such characters so strongly that in *The Last Tycoon* he went to all sorts of extra trouble trying to round out Cecilia's character, even though, from the nature of the story itself, it is hard to see how he could ever have contrived to keep her in the privileged position which mandarin criticism calls the point of view. The fact is that in this novel as in the others the reader is meant to be a detached spectator, with an intermediary between him and the action, remote from what goes on, curious and interested no doubt, but still uninvolved enough to be able to contemplate and moralize—never tempted to sit down in the road beside the wounded hero who points his machine gun at the spot where the Fascist tanks will momentarily

have to cross. This effect was important enough to Fitzgerald
to justify much effort. The effort's effect was, in large part,
to make the reader feel that he was from Minnesota, too.

The metaphor may well be dropped: for Minnesota read
Elsewhere. The time came when the kind of life Fitzgerald
had been writing about ceased to be exotic and became
familiar Elsewhere, everywhere. We may talk as much as we
like about the "proletarian thirties"; a simpler explanation
of the first public "rejection" of Fitzgerald is that everyone
got used to him, blasé.

So his first popularity collapsed when the public lost
interest in the kind of exotic materials he used because they
ceased to seem exotic. Bobbed hair became a convenience
and the flapper either rolled up her stockings or took them
off entirely in protest against the alarming aggressions of
Japan. To extend the scope of a perception of Alfred Kazin's,
the twenties had got tired of themselves. When Fitzgerald
returned to popularity, in the late forties and under the pro-
tecting auspices of Henry James, the climate had totally
changed; there was a new audience which had been too
young to know much of the twenties, for whom the era of
Prohibition and glitter was a Myth.

Even more than for his immediate contemporaries Fitzgerald had by then become a sort of Kilroy: wherever one
went he had been there, the omnipresent witness. He had
written about going to college—and when you got to college
yourself, his Princeton was the standard your college fell
short of. (Even Princeton fell short of Fitzgerald's Princeton,
it appears.) Also, you discovered, he knew the inside story
of the emancipated younger generation—and told it inordinately well. In brief, he was the man who had been to West
Egg—and even if you had lived on Long Island you might
never have seen West Egg long and steadily enough to see
it whole, and certainly not while it was still inhabited by the

mythical Very Rich. And he knew about life in Paris and in the villas you see as you whisk along the Corniche drive above the beaches from Golfe Juan to Menton. And about Hollywood. But, chiefly, he had known the twenties, which over the years have become one of the mistier areas of the American reality.

No one could be sorry that after years of an obscurity his work did not deserve Fitzgerald should have returned to general esteem, even though circumstances had as much to do with the reversal of fortune as did anything Fitzgerald ever had in the way of literary merit. He had the posthumous luck to fall into the hands of a very capable biographer; Arthur Mizener's book and the novel by Budd Schulberg fanned the spark which had been kept alive by critics like Edmund Wilson and Malcolm Cowley. From the time when the nation began to emerge from the socio-political binge of the thirties, it was only a question of how long it would take the public which reads books to catch up with documents like *The Crack-Up* and realize that dismissing Fitzgerald as a frivolous chronicler of frivolous parasites was a judgment in need of revising. One approves, possibly in a somewhat self-congratulatory glow of Anglo-Saxon fair play, of his recent popularity: *This Side of Paradise* is generally regarded as our best novel on the subject of going to college; *The Last Tycoon* is respected; *Tender Is the Night* and, even more, *The Great Gatsby* are recommended in college English courses; and while most of the short stories are forgotten, a number like "The Diamond as Big as the Ritz" are anthologized and force-fed to freshmen.

But one other circumstance which was influential in Fitzgerald's comeback seems to me unfortunate: the fact that he rode back into popularity on the recent wave of interest in literary craftsmanship. With the general success of the so-called New Criticism came the awareness that what chiefly differentiated writers like Hemingway, Faulkner, Wolfe, and Fitzgerald from their immediate predecessors like Sinclair Lewis and Dreiser was that they had a stronger sense of their professional obligations to the written work. Fitzgerald, however bad his personal relations with novelists like Edith Wharton, had shared the concern of the new-Jamesians with such matters as "point-of-view" and "composition in scenes"; and for critics who had assimilated the doctrines of Percy Lubbock and Joseph Warren Beach, no more could be needed—or perhaps even wanted. The James Revival had been on for ten years and had left a noticeable mark on the serious reading public. The age now demanded a novel animated by ethical concerns, and preferably one in which the action was refracted toward the reader by a "central moral consciousness," especially if it was written in "scenes." Such was the model James provided, and to critics who like to define fiction as "the ordering of events by the moral imagination," *The Great Gatsby*, in particular, commended itself highly. It had Nick Carraway at its center; it used "scenic technique"; it incited its reader to meditate on Values. Thus a very special conjunction of circumstances put *The Great Gatsby* in a higher niche than this novel may be expected to occupy now that the New Criticism has made its point, won its battle, and more or less retired from the wars.

For in style and in moral perceptiveness *The Great Gatsby* leaves much to be desired.

I wanted to get out and walk eastward toward the park through the *soft* twilight, but each time I tried to go I became entangled in some *wild*, strident argument which pulled me back, *as if with ropes,* into my chair. Yet *high over the city* our line of yellow windows must have contributed their share of human secrecy to the casual watcher in the *darkening* streets, and I was him, too, looking up and wondering. I was within and without, simultaneously enchanted and repelled by *the inexhaustible variety of life.* [Italics mine.]

These lines are typical: they contain one of the sudden, deep insights into a character, and through the character into himself, that Fitzgerald could bring off when he was at his best; and at the same time the prose itself is so fuzzy, and in a way so vulgar, that the insight is almost lost in what may be described very literally as the shuffle.

Nick's discovery that he is at once both spectator and participant is the insight, and since Nick is a projection of Fitzgerald's own personality the extension of the insight is automatic. Quite probably this paragraph is the origin of Malcolm Cowley's perception, which seems to me the most helpful any critic of Fitzgerald has yet given us, that Fitzgerald's writing has a double point of view—one that of the inured metropolitan who sees and knows everything and is always on the inside, and the other that of a wistful youngster from Minnesota who is on the outside looking in and wondering what everything is really all about. In any event it sums up both Nick's status in *The Great Gatsby* and Fitzgerald's role as novelist. And yet it is almost hidden by the kind of curious fumbling that goes on within a Fitzgerald sentence.

For in spite of the fundamentally deep perception, a great deal in the passage is simply not right. Why does the twilight have to be "soft"? What necessity makes the argument "wild" as well as "strident" and capable of pulling "as if with ropes"? What work is done by "high over the city"? Or by "darkening"? And, above all, why must he be enchanted by "the inexhaustible variety of life"? If they were alone in the passage we could pass by "soft" and "wild," since they are under very little stress and the eye slides easily by them; but "as if with ropes" is set off syntactically in its sentence and does stop the eye—and then it turns out that the eye has stopped for very little. "High over the city" isn't even true of the physical situation, for the strident party is taking place in an ordinary apartment house at about the same height from the ground as most of the apartment houses of a city that happens to be built on the vertical; it merely echoes a stereotype of the pseudo-poetry of the Metropolis. "Darkening" probably would not bother us by itself, but in the context, following "soft" twilight and the yellow-lighted windows, it joins in creating the effect of low-priced poetry. And finally, ending the terminal sentence of a paragraph that builds to it as to a climax, comes the egregious cliché—that Fitzgerald must have been the millionth person to write—about "the inexhaustible variety of life."

I am ready to affirm that there are more lapses like those just noted in *The Great Gatsby* than in his later novels, but the later ones are by no means free of them. Witness the following from *Tender Is the Night:*

The studio manager opened a small door in a blank wall of a stage building and with sudden, glad familiarity Rosemary followed him into half darkness. Here and there figures spotted the twilight, *turning up ashen faces to her like souls in purgatory watching the passage of a mortal through.* There were whispers and soft voices and, apparently from afar, the gentle tremolo of a small organ. Turning the corner made by some flats, they came upon the white crackling glow of a stage, where a French actor—his shirt front, collar, and cuffs tinted a brilliant pink— and an American actress stood motionless face to face. They stared at each other with dogged eyes, as though they had been in the same position for hours; and still for a long time nothing happened, no one moved. A bank of lights went off with a savage hiss, went on again; the *plaintive* tap of a hammer *begged admission to nowhere in the distance;* a blue face appeared among the blinding lights above, called something unintelligible into the upper blackness. Then the silence was broken by a voice in front of Rosemary.

Once again the italics are mine. They tell their own story.

The "feel" of the studio comes home here with an immediacy such as few of Fitzgerald's contemporaries ever contrive, largely because of the palpable authenticity of the color-impressions: the blue face above, the pale faces below, the pink in the actor's costume, the "crackling" white of the lights on the stage, the intensity of the lights in general—conveyed, curiously, almost as much to the ear as to the eye. This is the kind of writing that the word authenticity was invented for. And yet, right in the midst of everything, the ashen faces and the hammer . . . Fitzgerald just cannot let well enough alone, cannot resist the temptation to use more qualifiers than he needs.

In a time when writers are so intent on rendering exact sensations, and bent upon emphasizing each sensation's uniqueness, overqualification is a widely shared habit and we are justified in taking it to be a characteristic trait of the period's style rather than a fault. Faulkner heaps up his homemade adjectives and adverbs until the effect is dizzying. But there is a signal difference: each of them—when Faulkner is at his best—really qualifies and changes the total appearance of the thing it affects, whereas Fitzgerald's sometimes add nothing but length to the sentence. And so Fitzgerald's writing is not always what his friend Hemingway liked to call "clean, and hard, and true." Hemingway's notion was that if every element in a sentence was there out of a dynamic necessity, then the writing had "integrity." Evident correspondence with some internal necessity is precisely what Fitzgerald so often lacks.

Statistics could be made which would show that he lacked it less often in *Tender Is the Night* than in *The Great Gatsby*, and this is one of my reasons for regretting that the latter should be the one which inevitably springs to the public mind upon the mention of his name. *The Great Gatsby* marks

an intermediate stage in Fitzgerald's development. One
gathers from Edmund Wilson and from Mizener's biography
that he arrived late at complete literacy: the story is that
his early attempts at writing were incredibly bad and that
he learned better only by making all the mistakes that were
to be made. He had the luck to have men like Wilson and
John Peale Bishop, and, later, Maxwell Perkins, to point them
out, and the patience and humility to profit from such help.
But there is one kind of bad writing that not even the legen-
dary Perkins could "edit out," because it is inherent in the
writer's conception of his subject, which is another way of
saying inherent in his native taste. Only as the individual's
taste improves, through some kind of self-imposed discipline,
does the style purify itself. And there is every evidence that
this happened in Fitzgerald's case.

But it had not happened when he wrote *The Great
Gatsby:*

The quiet lights in the houses were humming out into the
darkness and there was a stir and bustle among the stars.
Out of the corner of his eye Gatsby saw that the blocks of
the sidewalks really formed a ladder and mounted to a secret
place above the trees—he could climb to it, if he climbed alone,
and once there he could suck on the pap of life, gulp down
the incomparable milk of wonder.

His heart beat faster and faster as Daisy's white face came
up to his own. He knew that when he kissed this girl, and
forever wed his unutterable visions to her perishable breath,
his mind would never romp again like the mind of God. So he
waited, listening for a moment longer to the tuning-fork that
had been struck upon a star. Then he kissed her. At his lips'
touch she blossomed for him like a flower and the incarnation
was complete.

Through all he said, even through his appalling sentimentality,
I was reminded of something—an elusive rhythm, a fragment
of lost words, that I had heard somewhere a long time ago.
For a moment a phrase tried to take shape in my mouth and

my lips parted like a dumb man's, as though there was more struggling upon them than a wisp of startled air. But they made no sound, and what I had almost remembered was uncommunicable forever.

These streets that change their dimension and become rungs of a ladder to the stars, this pap of life that gives off the milk of wonder, the wedding of unutterable vision to perishable breath, the wisp of air struggling on the man's lips, are empty and pretentious; something shallow is trying to sound as if it were deep. To use Hemingway's word, it is phony.

We can get pretty clearly at why, at such moments as this, Hemingway seems so much Fitzgerald's superior. The difference lies in each man's relation to his audience. Hemingway wrote with such admirable unity of tone because he thought of his readers as a homogeneous group. The taste that underlies his prose may displease many, but at least it is a single taste; even when he exaggerates the characteristics of his style until he sounds like a parody of himself, as I think he does in *To Have and Have Not*, the unity of taste is still present. Both *The Sun Also Rises* and *The Torrents of Spring* were written for a small group of initiates who already knew the language and the basic emotions, and would understand inexplicit references. Then and later, as the many side remarks in *Death in the Afternoon* testify, Hemingway was willing to exclude from his audience readers who, he felt, did not belong to it and were not keyed to understand his language. If it is true that he told someone that *Across the River and Into the Trees* was written "for us old bastards," the remark is very much in point here. So are his many more or less derisive comments about critics: in Hemingway's mind, many of them just were outside the circle that he wanted to reach.

Fitzgerald did not lack the talent it takes to get a similar unity of tone. There are plenty of pages, even in *The Great Gatsby*, so clearly keyed to the internal necessities, so "clean, and hard, and true," that there can be no question of his ability to write prose "of integrity." But at the point in history when the editors of the *New Yorker* were making epochal announcement that their magazine would not be written and edited for "the old lady from Dubuque," and every number of Mencken's *American Mercury* was heaping slurs on the Middle West, Fitzgerald was writing for an audience which may have included the old lady herself and certainly took in her half-emancipated daughters. This need not mean—and I don't mean—that Fitzgerald pandered deliberately to a taste which demanded that paragraphs end with soggy phrases about the infinite variety of life. Mizener's biography shows what a conscientious workman he was and just how much he wanted to avoid that kind of pandering. But he was caught in a sort of trap, and he knew it.

On the last page of the notes which Edmund Wilson published with *The Last Tycoon* appear two very revealing items: first, "Tragedy of these men was that nothing in their lives had really bitten deep at all. Bald Hemingway characters"; and second, "Don't wake the Tarkington ghosts." From the two notes we have only to abstract the names of the two novelists. There was a taste abroad with which were identified writers like Tarkington, just as there was also a taste, then forming though not fully formed, for writing reflecting the more rigid standards of men like Hemingway. The broad American audience Fitzgerald wrote for shared both in varying proportions, and Fitzgerald shared them, too. It was implicit both in his subject matter and in the stance he assumed toward it that he should do so.

We have spoken of the elegiac sensibility which persisted in middle western realism well after its practitioners had become the most significant group writing fiction in America. How deeply and thoroughly such a mode of feeling pervades a particular ethos could be the subject of a long and perhaps interesting study. To get at it one would have to pay much attention to what is read in the early grades of schools, to Sunday school manuals, children's magazines, instruction books for teachers, family pages of newspapers, etc., to catch the reflection of what people in given localities thought was good for their young. All I can do here is assert that one could not escape the influence merely by coming east to Princeton after a middle western childhood. Fitzgerald brought some of it with him, obviously. And I suspect that its presence in his writing may be the indirect reason why, in the long run, American criticism will not go on considering him the really fine craftsman it has taken him to be in recent years.

For the issue of style is central in the structure of *The Great Gatsby* because it creates the voice of the "central moral consciousness." In other words, it is the principal means of characterizing Nick Carraway. Fitzgerald has been justly praised for the invention of the Carraway character. The strategy of telling the story through the awareness of a man who has his own independent life going on all the while —his job to do, his off-stage love affair to terminate, his private concerns at West Egg—greatly intensifies what Henry James would have called the "felt life" of the story. As his connection with the main action grows closer, more or less despite his own preferences, the novel develops a dimension of density as palpable as what Conrad achieves in the stories which are told through the character of Marlowe, combined with a kind of naturalness Conrad hardly tried to manage. To have brought him off so well is enough to put Fitzgerald in that small category of novelists who really know what they are doing. But there still remains the question whether Nick Carraway is the central moral consciousness this novel needed to satisfy the rather stringent demands of a criticism which requires, in addition to structural perfection, real depth of moral perception.

Nick is not supposed to be a fool. He has had what his father calls "the advantages": an attentive bringing-up and a Yale education. War and peace have given him opportunity to observe people under stress. He has at least normal social experience and social acumen. At thirty he is quite representative of the kind of American who has had most of the privileges his country has to offer. Moreover, his heart is in the right place; his emotions are warm and easily stirred; he is capable of separating his loyalties from his peculiar personal interests. But it must be added that he has more compassion than brains. He is unable to feel and think, at the same time, about the matter at hand.

His feelings eventually tell him that something is very wrong and put him very firmly on the side of Gatsby, this man of whom, he makes it very clear, he does not "approve." He does not believe the story Gatsby tells about the war and Oxford, but as he listens his "incredulity" becomes submerged in "fascination." He knows perfectly well that Gatsby's secretiveness about his business is shady, but even after he meets Meyer Wolfsheim, the man who bought the Black Sox, he never quite gets it through his head that Gatsby is not only a successful but also a cheap crook. Just as he realizes with no great effort that Jordan Baker is "incurably dishonest" without the fact's "making any difference" to him—he is just "casually sorry"—he lets Gatsby's crookedness make no difference to him by seeing it, through a curtain of sentimentality, as an instrument for attaining what Nick regularly calls "the Dream."

So far as Nick is concerned, we never find out just exactly what the Dream is. Every time the subject comes up, he slides off into gooey sentiment.

Almost five years! There must have been moments even that afternoon when Daisy tumbled short of his dreams—not through her own fault, but because of the colossal vitality of his illusion. It had gone beyond her, beyond everything. He had thrown himself into it with a creative passion, adding to it all the time, decking it out with every bright feather that drifted his way. No amount of fire or freshness can challenge what a man will store up in his ghostly heart.

But the more inkling one gets of what the Dream consists of, the more clearly one sees that surely it is nothing very pretty. James Gatz, the farm boy from Minnesota, gets the notion he can have all the gratifications he wants if only he will work hard enough. These gratifications come to sum themselves up in the person of Daisy, who eventually marries Tom Buchanan. Gatsby retains her, even so, as an emblem of his acquisitive drive. But this drive, we remember, was formed before he ever saw Daisy. "So he invented," Nick tells us, "just the sort of Jay Gatsby a seventeen-year-old boy would be likely to invent, and to this conception he was faithful to the end." This comes down to saying, simply, that Gatsby's career was the result of putting the lethal powers of a ruthless man at the service of an adolescent wish-fulfilment. He emerges as a case of arrested development, of juvenile delinquency physically grown up.

But the power of Gatsby's dream blinds Nick to the obvious and his sense of fair play also confuses issues. From people like Tom and Daisy Gatsby has had a bad deal. " 'They're a rotten crowd,' I shouted across the lawn. 'You're worth the whole damn bunch put together.' " He adds in the next paragraph that this was the only compliment he ever gave Gatsby, because he "disapproved of him from beginning to end." Possibly the compliment should not be considered a very great one, since it compared Gatsby with people of no high moral quality; but Nick has just said, also, that Gatsby was following some sort of Grail, which is a strong enough expression in the circumstances to make it clear that Nick is not aware of his own moral ambivalence.

Nick's sincerity is unexceptionable. He is deeply disturbed by Gatsby's disaster; it becomes his own. Gatsby's death ends a chapter in his own life: he gives up his house, sells his car to the grocer, quits his job, sees Tom and Jordan one last time, and then takes his "provincial squeamishness" back to his home in the Middle West—thus tacking something typically American on a novel which, in general pattern, belongs to the category whose prototype is Balzac's *Lost Illusions*. His dream, as well as Gatsby's, has been shattered—and he finally identifies himself with the myriad young men who have left the shelter of home to discover that life is not so enchanting as they have been brought up to expect. What makes this particular version of a familar theme so specifically American is his laying blame on his having passed from one cultural area to another. Fitzgerald's reader will agree that something in Nick's development has prevented his reaching the moral maturity which would have allowed him to perceive Gatsby's "appalling sentimentality" without falling away into sentimentality himself—as we have seen him do in this prose, which is not only Fitzgerald's style but also Nick's characterizing utterance.

In the famous article on Flaubert, Henry James deplores that the master should have placed in the center of *Madame Bovary* and *The Sentimental Education* such "mean" moral consciences as Emma Bovary and Frédéric Moreau. To call Nick Carraway "mean" would be manifestly unfair, but there would be nothing unfair in calling him inadequate for the job. At thirty he is still too young for the moral responsibility it involves.

A final estimate of Fitzgerald has to include the fact of his preferring such immature characters for the point

of view. Rosemary turns eighteen in *Tender Is the Night;*
Cecilia is no more than twenty and still an undergraduate
at Bennington. At thirty, Nick shares their disadvantage.
What each of them is busy trying to pick through is not the
surface of an ethically complex situation but the eggshell of
his own emotional and social inexperience. The distance
which separates such instruments of the moral imagination
from one on the order of Lambert Strether is vertiginous.

All this suggests that Fitzgerald falls somewhat short
of the eminence as moralist which recent criticism would
like to attribute to him. Actually, there is some reason to
doubt that Fitzgerald was really devoted to the use of the
central moral consciousness as such; i.e., he used it, but not
especially for the purposes of the moralist. From his notes
and scenarios for *The Last Tycoon* it is clear that he meant
originally to have Cecilia narrate the action and thus rigidly
restrict the point of view, but it is also clear from the
finished parts of the book that this strategy did not appeal
to him strongly enough to cause him to rebuild his story
in a way that would make its use plausible. Similarly,
Rosemary serves as point of view character in only a
relatively small section of *Tender Is the Night,* after which
she becomes merely another member of the novel's population. One has to conclude that if the temporarily central
position of these characters was important to Fitzgerald,
the reason for the importance has no connection with moral
observation. For such a character to be a useful means of
indirect moral analysis he would have, obviously, to maintain
his privileged position throughout the story, the end of which
should be at least as morally significant as the beginning.

Nick's inability to break through the murk and see Gatsby
for what he really is—a pitiable romantic oaf—and his missing
the fundamental preposterousness of the yarn about the
poor boy who beat his way to fortune for love of the girl

who spurned him, and then got killed for his pains, is probably indistinguishable from Fitzgerald's. It does not seem to have perturbed many among his audience, and I suspect the reason is that most of his audience do not take Fitzgerald to be a moralist at all. They take Gatsby's career as being all of a piece with the sensibility which did not object to ending a paragraph with a cliché about life's inexhaustible variety.

For its proper purpose, that sensibility is a perfectly useful one. But the purpose has to do not with morals but with manners. It was because Fitzgerald was dealing essentially with manners that he could work so hard on the "central" characters of two of his novels, only to let them drop back out of their central positions. Their role was to introduce the reader to, and ease him into, a new strange world; once he was acclimated their importance declined. They were there to help him report the "feel" of a certain kind of life, the precise sensation of it. And because, after all, "felt life" is a synonym for "novel," we honor Fitzgerald's achievement.

But we should not honor it beyond measure, for the matter of manners and morals is not necessarily the ultimate one. There still remains the question whether Fitzgerald did "feel" what was truly there to be felt—a question of authenticity. It has to be raised on two planes—the plane of literal accuracy and the plane of symbol. For Fitzgerald did willy-nilly create a symbol in *The Great Gatsby,* other than that very obvious and not very useful one of the billboard eyeglasses which leer across the ashheaps at the dramatis personae; and it is a symbol so central to his view of life that its influence extends beyond the limits of the book in which he creates it and becomes the presiding symbol of most of his work. This is the Big Party.

As a symbol it stands for a whole attitude toward life. It is also a fact of cultural history. And a very considerable part of Fitzgerald's worth as a novelist is determined by how he dealt with it both as fact and as symbol. By the record we shall have to conclude that his treatment of both fact and symbol was inadequate, but also that its inadequacy was foreordained by the circumstances which made him a transplant trying to understand and explain other transplants.

On the level of literal truth, Fitzgerald's report is, undeniably, suspect.

By definition the Big Party has to be a standard part of the legend of the Jazz Age: no party, no jazz; the twenties had not acquired the curious habit of listening to dance music while standing motionless. And thus Gatsby, who gave the biggest and loudest ones, those models no party since has come up to, becomes a standard part also. Everybody knows this.

But, strangely, it is passing difficult to find anyone who knows it at first hand. The historian, born too late—though not by much—tries conscientiously to find among his elders one who was ever present at anything like the sterile orgies at West Egg, but tries mostly in vain. Everyone has heard about Caresse Crosby but at several removes, and they can all tell you how at the end of one night on the town Scott Fitzgerald, or else Zelda, one or both, tried a swim in a public fountain. Some admit they don't know what such parties were like; a few give the impression that they know but won't talk; most end by suggesting that probably the best way to get an idea is to read Fitzgerald's books!

As a sourcebook on the mores of a time *The Great Gatsby* is consequently of questionable value. On the face of the evidence, there cannot have been the number of real Lease-Breakers we assume. If there had been, Fitzgerald would have had to write a different book, because the one he did write is a story about a man who threw great parties, addressed to a reading audience willing to believe that such things happened but unfamiliar with the actual festivities. And the plot would have had to be different, because with stupendous riots going on all over the place, Gatsby, dumb as he may have been, would hardly have expected another one to bait Daisy back into his Dream.

The glitterglamour legend of the Prohibition Era would obviously be much poorer without the bacchanalian element, but there was doubtless never much danger that the legend would die out. We have always persisted in believing in it, if for no better reason than that the most palpably imaginative and hypercolored accounts make far better reading than the sober, documented studies which, if taken seriously, would compromise the legend beyond recognition. And besides, we needed greatly to believe in them, because the legend of the twenties is less the work of the twenties than of the next decade. Since, once the great awakening of the social conscience had come, the recent past had to be repudiated, logically it had to be horrendous enough to be worth repudiating. There had to have been enough frivolity for people to feel satisfactorily guilty or indignant about.

Actually, in the cold light of criticism Gatsby is somewhat harder to believe in than Achilles or Grendel. It is not too harsh to call him an oaf, since only an oaf could have harbored the particular set of illusions which Nick Carraway sentimentalizes as the Dream. But besides having a low I.Q., he has the disadvantage of being an unusually implausible version of the educated freebooter living magnificently and conspicuously by operations beyond the reach of the law. At least, the newspapers of the time are categorical on the point: the really big men of the underworld did not make a practice of calling public attention to themselves, and kept to a minimum the amount of their business with those who did. One such individual was bad for everybody's trade; the surprise is not that Gatsby got rubbed out, but that he got it from an angry garage-keeper rather than from a gunsel delegated to make sure that important secrets were kept permanently safe. It is even difficult to think that true Bigtimers exposed themselves to the gunfire of outraged husbands.

The tremendous brawls Gatsby staged at West Egg brought people who did not know each other into one place for the purposes of feeding, making love, getting drunk, and having a hell of a time generally. Obviously the anonymity had a special charm: the guests might have notoriety if not distinction; the girl who did something alcoholically indiscreet might possibly be a rising starlet, the man with her either a director or the trigger-man of some gang; those uninterested in food, love, or booze could amuse themselves watching other people's antics— something to tell their friends about. Or just wander purposelessly about. Just about everybody, sooner or later, gets lost.

Nick's first and principal impression, it should be noted, is one of unreality. People float up to him out of the dark, say or do something unexpected, float away again. Past him go people looking for people, or trying to get away from people. Husbands are separated from their wives, or wish they could be. Groups form for a moment and break up again. Semi-resident drunks wander about the house where they have camped from week end to week end. Guests wonder audibly who their host is and what he does, and explain to each other why they are there, poor spectators for a ritual of conspicuous consumption—since such rituals require spectators who have names and faces—but excellent though involuntary performers in a tremendous masquerade. And meanwhile Gatsby himself moves about on the periphery, as indifferent to the crowd as they to him, the wistful creator of a fantastic temporary world, waiting for his miracle to happen.

The more one contemplates the spectacle, the surer one gets that to believe all this one had better be from Elsewhere. Of those two visions Fitzgerald is supposed to have exploited simultaneously, the knowing one and the wistful-outsider one, the second is dominant. And so, ultimately we do not believe what we are told. We merely believe that the Great Party looked like this to a transplant. As literal truth we won't have it.

But there are other truths to tell besides the literal one, and so we try taking the Great Party as symbol. This means taking it in relation to Gatsby's famous Dream, toward which Nick Carraway's disposition is so disastrously ambivalent. There would have been no parties if James Gatz had not wandered away from Minnesota, into a war, and eventually into Louisville. There he met Daisy, and trouble came. Imagine yourself Gatsby. You find yourself in another place from those you know. You have been given special, attractive clothes (i.e., the uniform of an officer) such as you have never had, and you are different yourself; and a girl who somewhere else might never have looked at you turns out to love you, at least for the shining moment. Then somebody—in Washington—waves a wand and you ship out. Poetry has very abruptly changed to prose.

And so those parties he gives, after the war, in his cardboard castle on Long Island, in the hope of getting Daisy at least to come back into his life enough for him to see her, are Gatsby's attempt to recover the poetry. This seems almost too obvious to be worth saying, but recasting the whole situation in such terms makes it possible to place the symbol in its tradition.

Actually the tradition is an old one and got to America only after a long European career. Symbolist-Idealist dogma has always included the tenet that there must be some sort of life, somewhere, which is better than the tarnished and degraded variety available to the human adult. The life of the grownup was alleged to be totally inferior to what his own childhood and youth had allowed him to expect. The assumption of the *toga virilis* was a disappointing experience, against which it was only logical to protest. In the literature which grew up in France around this theme, the Big Party emerged as perhaps the commonest of symbols.

"Life, if I remember rightly," wrote Rimbaud at the beginning of *A Season in Hell*, "used to be a Great Party where all hearts were opened and every wine flowed free." He has lost the key to this fete, he adds, and would do anything to find it again. And in the rest of *A Season in Hell*, the only book Rimbaud cared enough for to send it to the printer, he returns repeatedly to his refrain.

It is obvious that Rimbaud means that some paradisiac moment lay already behind him. He was still under twenty, but the Great Party was in the past. Yet his biography, as we know it, hardly allows the conclusion that, after puberty, the poet experienced much recognizable happiness. Most of the time he was trying to get away from a repressive mother and their home in a monstrously dull provincial town, or was lost in the poverty and squalor which were his fate once he contrived to make good his escape. I suspect that what he means by the *Grand Festin* was the brief period when his poetic powers were at their height, in late 1871 and early 1872. They were extremely precocious, and had probably begun to wane by the time he dropped writing in verse and turned to the prose of the *Illuminations*. It seems probable that he associated his poetic vigor with

a kind of childish purity which he had proceeded, early
and conspicuously, to lose. Some of his more self-assured
interpreters would even like to believe that some "Myth of
Childhood" underlies most of his work: "The Drunken Boat"
would, for them, be about the passage from childhood to
adult status and about his regret over the loss involved.
What is clear to everyone is that he did react against
having to grow up, and that in his expression of his feelings
the symbol of the Big Party—what he called *Le Grand Festin*
—played a conspicuous role.

First in poetry, but gradually invading prose as the grip
of Naturalism upon the French novel loosened, the situation
of the adolescent came to preoccupy an impressive number
of French writers, and the Big Party, in one form or another,
maintained its privileged position. Proust, Gide, Martin du
Gard, Schlumberger, Lacretelle, Henri Alain-Fournier, and
Jean Giraudoux are the best known of a list of names which
would include novelists by the dozen. The most explicit
novel, and thus the most useful here, is Alain-Fournier's
Le Grand Meaulnes, known in English translation as
The Wanderer.

Superficially this book has so little in common with
The Great Gatsby that a comparison of the two seems most
unlikely. Meaulnes is a big boy in a country school in France
who goes to sleep while driving a horse to meet the daily
train at a rail point some miles away. His horse takes a wrong
fork and Meaulnes awakes in an unfamiliar landscape. He
goes on, hoping to find help; night falls; his horse goes
lame, and, while its driver is asking directions at a lonely
farmhouse, wanders off by itself. Meaulnes goes on on foot,
stumbling in darkness until he comes on a large estate and
crawls into one of the buildings to take cover for the night.
He seems to be expected; friendly servants give him strange
but pleasant clothes, and he joins a party, already in

progress, where only children are present except for one
girl who is very lovely and about his own age. For two
days he forgets everything else, swept off on the tide of
an unknown pleasure. Then, suddenly, everyone is packed
into wagons and driven off; in the dark Meaulnes cannot
see the country he passes through, and when at last he
is set down near the village he comes from he has no idea
where he has been.

Alain-Fournier was close enough to the Symbolist tradition to be haunted by the possibility of "another landscape,"
a realm of being which we almost touch but never get
to see clear. Meaulnes is one of those rare youngsters
who by luck manage to cross the dividing line, though
only for a moment. That we are confronted by an archetype
here is inescapable; this is the Young Knight on his first
adventure who loses himself, loses his horse, is hurt, is
helped by simple dwellers in the wild, and after further
vicissitudes comes to a Miraculous Castle where pleasure
and the lovely maiden wait. Pure, lovely poetry!

Now, leave out the archetypal trappings and for Meaulnes
read Gatsby. One life momentarily exchanged for another.
The new clothes. The perpetual party. The girl. And then
the sudden parting and an immense, yearning desire to
return. Poetry again. Anyone, anywhere, would recognize
it immediately for what it is—anyone except, apparently, one
lone man.

Gatsby. For just here the two stories diverge. Meaulnes
searches for his lost domain and his Yvonne until at last he
finds them. And when he finds them he discovers also
that all the glamour has gone. He has grown up. Poetry has
given up its place to prose. For Gatsby, on the other hand,
the glamour never evaporates. His Big Party re-creates, as
best it can, that lovely evanescent moment in Louisville,
and even after he has found Daisy again and had a good

look at her he does not get the idea. He never becomes able to distinguish between poetry and prose.

For this reason there is no real pathos in *The Great Gatsby*. Gatsby cannot make the essential distinction; if such understanding resided anywhere it would have to be in Nick. Alain-Fournier's book profits by a wiser choice of point of view. Little Seurel, the son of Meaulnes' teacher and the larger boy's boon companion, through whom we see the story, moves from complete bafflement to a final understanding of what has happened—which, it seems, he arrives at even before Meaulnes does. The story, narrated retrospectively, is told in the tone of someone who has discovered the real meaning of the events. He recognizes, when he sees it, an inevitable part of life and this, after all, is the meaning of the central symbol. Nick Carraway, in contrast, simply concludes that the dramatis personae have all suffered from having wandered too far from home.

The principal moral of this story is not that it is better, for a writer, to come from French Sologne than from the upper Middle West. It is simply that it is better to be able to distinguish prose from poetry, poetry from prose. If we have to conclude that being from the Middle West rendered the distinction difficult to make, then we must recognize that a writer like Fitzgerald has certain special traps to avoid. In connection with Lionel Trilling's understanding of writers like Dreiser, I have drawn attention to the curious elegiac mood into which many midwestern "realists" tend to sink whenever the context calls for a display of emotion. From *Spoon River* to the image of the maudlin Old Champ which Ernest Hemingway offered the public from time to time, we have had any amount of this peculiarly inadequate sensibility. Gatsby's failure, which is also Nick Carraway's and which in turn is Fitzgerald's, would appear to be closely akin to it.

There would, of course, have been another way to approach the Great Party. Ever since *The Great Gatsby* was first published there have been periodical efforts to see it as a contemporary *Satyricon*. Now that Petronius' little gem, long inaccessible to many because of the hard Latin and the mincing translations, is at hand in the racy English of William Arrowsmith, any reader who likes may try the idea for size. What he will discover is that Scott Fitzgerald was no Petronius.

Trimalchio shares with Jay Gatsby the condition of having more money than taste and the faith that enough lavish display will make him admired. But right here the comparison ends. Trimalchio had Petronius and Petronius, whoever he was and whatever he was—and however de-praved—was also a Roman gentleman who knew his way about town, and what was properly done and what wasn't. His taste is absolutely secure. There is, in the *Satyricon*, not the least wondering on the part of the narrator where anybody stands, or what this fantastic extravaganza adds up to. Nor does Petronius leave the reader in any doubt as to the nature of the narrator and his companion. He simply exercises his satirist's right to assume that his reader shares his own general social attitudes. For a sat-irist this is just about the essential minimum.

And here and now it becomes luminously clear why *The Great Gatsby* should not be taken as satire. Satire assumes an understanding on the part of the reader which Fitzgerald's novel may not—a reasonable familiarity with the human foibles which it exposes. Satirizing something one's audience does not know runs just as much chance of success as parodying a totally unfamiliar poem. *The Great Gatsby* comes no closer to being satire than would a *Satyricon* written by a recent arrival from Transalpine Gaul.

If there were no other guide available, the obviousness

of the reason why *The Great Gatsby* should not be read as satire would be enough to point out the appropriate attitude to take toward this book and in some measure toward all Fitzgerald's books. As a moralist he suffers from an inability to find a solid position of his own. As a novelist of manners he merits complete respect in so far as his report can be credited; but there is a point beyond which crediting it becomes extremely difficult. As a stylist he is often admirable, but there are moments when his difficulties with manners and morals corrupt his style. There is always the "but," the qualification of the praise, and each time we pronounce it we return to the subject of displacement in America, the effect on our writing of the universal problem of cultural adjustment.

On the other hand, none of these considerations diminishes him with respect to the accomplishment for which we should, and possibly do, honor him most. He made the great myths of his time—the myth of going to college, the myth of the unhappy expatriate, the myth of the Jazz Age itself. He had help, of course, but he was still the principal contributor. The debt we owe him is the one we acknowledge to those writers, rarely more than two or three in each generation, who help us understand ourselves in relation to our time. To merit this it was no obstacle to him to be a transplant, a displaced person writing about other displaced persons. Probably being such was an advantage. Possibly it was even the one indispensable condition.

4

Cozzens and His Critics:
A Problem in Perspective

THREE OF James Gould Cozzens' last four novels are set in relatively small communities situated well off the beaten track, where progress is slow and change hardly distinguishable from decay. And because he sees such places for what they are, Cozzens explores a kind of American life which the ordinary run of novelists do not touch. The characters in *Men and Brethren,* in *The Just and the Unjust,* and even more in *By Love Possessed* live in the unhappy assurance that almost any change that overtakes them will be for the worse, because their own status is entirely dependent upon, and identifiable with, the status quo.

Their ancestors made these communities what they are and in turn the communities have made the descendants what they cannot help being. Characteristically they tend to equate the welfare of the body politic with their own and subscribe to a set of values which is bound to reserve them a special place. This does not make them particularly lovely, and there is no doubt at all that, as has been said, Arthur Winner, Jr. is at times an insufferable prig as well as conservative, middle-aged, and middle-class. His moral crisis comes from his being so thoroughly what his community has made him that when the chips are down he has no moral resources; all the unhappy events which lead

up to the discovery of Noah Tuttle's defalcations lead also
to Winner's having to agree to hide what his partner has
done. There is no out because there is no life for him outside
the town. Where could he go? Where but here could he be
anything?

Many of his critics have been distressed that Cozzens
should feel, and reveal, sympathy for characters like Arthur
Winner. I have to agree that there are times when I share
their feeling. But just because of the relationship between
Winner and his community, a good share of the critical
disapproval is misplaced: the critic, who is a product of
one kind of American culture, looks upon a character
who is the product of another kind—and scorns the character
when, if he could only see it, what really repels him is the
other culture. Or, to return to an old refrain, things are
not always seen clearest when seen from New York.

Such a fault in perspective seems to underlie the famous
hatchet job by Dwight Macdonald called "By Cozzens
Possessed," which made almost a collector's item of
Commentary for January, 1958. Possibly Macdonald's name
would not be writ very large on a final listing of the critics
who now practice in America. He is less a critic than a
polygraph operating on the periphery of intellectual journal-
ism, an essayist notable chiefly for writing knowledgeably
on an amazing variety of subjects, from how much to tip
in restaurants and the vagaries of Norman Mailer to why
he does not intend to vote in a presidential election; he
is one of those chronic insiders who always have the late
dope. Much of his life has been spent around magazines, the
names of which mark points on the trajectory of a career:
Exeter *Monthly,* Yale *Lit, Miscellany, Partisan Review, Politics,* the *New Yorker.* It is a career which would be inconceivable for anyone who was not willing to plant himself in
New York indefinitely, or to adopt the local angle of vision.

Amid the din of applause raised by the reviewers of the dailies and weeklies, who gave *By Love Possessed* something more than its full meed, Macdonald raised the always relevant question about the emperor's clothes. The book was, he declared, a dismal swamp of clumsy and pretentious writing. He was not the only one to say so, of course, but he was easily the most vociferous, and he quoted samples until his point was made beyond cavil—as well as beyond endurance. He was right. When writing is bad there should always be someone ready to say—perhaps to shout—that it is nothing short of terrible. There should also be someone, of course, to ask whether, in a long novel, bad writing makes a really momentous difference. The number of "bad" writers—bad according to the standards of their time—who have written great novels is almost exactly equal to the number of great novels that have been written. But let this pass, and score the round for Macdonald. It is something of a pity that he did not leave the ring while he was ahead.

It has been hinted that he was less annoyed by *By Love Possessed* than by the inordinate and unmeasured praise it was getting from the reviewers. At the point in his article where he has to record that the sale has gone over 170,000 copies he sounds close to apoplectic. Surely some of his irritation was unnecessary; we are not obliged to accept his view that our professional reviewers are a collection of resolutely malicious dolts. Reviewers have their troubles with perspective, too: if you swim forever against a stream of infrequently relieved mediocrity, as they do, anything better than mediocre is likely to look quite superior indeed, and the price of having to work as fast as they do in the nature of their job is that every so often they make mistakes. In spite of Elizabeth Hardwick in the supplement on American writing in *Harper's* for October, 1959, we are just about as well informed on the subject of current writing as are the French, whose larger literary press is also shallower; and if our reviewers are sometimes indecisive as compared with the English, at least we are not forever having pseudo-authoritative and arbitrary opinion crammed down our throats. But in the final count, it was good for Macdonald to strike out at the quality of the reviewing just as it was good for him to lament Cozzens' prose. The reviewers had, after all, gone all the way overboard for a book which on closer examination turned out to be visibly less arresting than *War and Peace*, or *Moby Dick*, or even its own immediate predecessor in the Cozzens canon, *Guard of Honor*. But it was not a good sign that he should turn purple in the face.

For it is clear in his article that Macdonald's violence was also stirred by the feeling that this novel had been written for "middlebrows," and that its commercial success was a middlebrow phenomenon. On this subject he is again right: there would be too few with brows higher than middle at large in the land to buy 170,000 of any book if they each took several apiece, and it was hardly necessary to adduce the evidence that the late Bernard DeVoto, whose preference for the middlebrow was immovable, once thought Cozzens a considerable novelist.

What Macdonald forgot is that by right of birth the novel is blatantly middlebrow anyhow. It became respectable only when the Industrial Revolution brought forward a new class with money to buy books, leisure to read them, and too little old-fashioned classical education to support prejudices in taste. Before that it had been a minor genre, fit mostly to amuse women and others who were not up to anything better. Afterward, with the help of steam presses, inexpensive paper, and more adhesive printer's ink, it gradually took over until not even the theater could compete with it. Its authors have regularly been middlebrows themselves, and the remark of some other critic which Macdonald objects to so contemptuously, that Cozzens is a writer rather than a literary gent, has been ascribed to almost every American novelist of stature from Mark Twain to Faulkner and Hemingway—all of them having said it of themselves. Even the most determined blue-stocking makes some concessions to Philistine taste when he takes up the novel form. What is wonderful is that now and then some novel achieves greatness within the limits that the form itself imposes.

What Macdonald was getting at was that the whole system of values in *By Love Possessed,* those a man like Arthur Winner, Jr. would live by, are also such as the middlebrow would hold and as would appeal to middle-brow readers. No doubt he is right again. But again he is somewhat beside the point. The charge brought against any novel of embodying the wrong values makes sense only so long as the tone of the book remains immediately contemporary; as soon as history moves forward enough so that there is no longer a conflict between the code which the novelist treats as valid and some other code which is held by a considerable number of the novelist's fellow-citizens, the whole criticism evaporates. Just how many of the novels we call great propose ways of living their readers would consider adopting today? One may doubt very much that the major works of Stendhal, Jane Austen, Henry James, or Joseph Conrad would make the list. And what about the grotesque snobbery which informs the monumental novel of Marcel Proust without, apparently, making it unpalatable for most readers?

It is not surprising that, as Macdonald's article goes on, his target shifts from Cozzens' book to Cozzens himself. This brings us much nearer the crux of the whole argument. The author, as Macdonald sketches him, is just about as unsatisfactory as his book. We are given a column or so of documentary evidence of how Cozzens feels about Negroes, the Republican party, life in New York and in Virginia, and his Tory ancestors—plus some unpleasant remark or other the novelist is reported to have made about his Jewish wife who, Macdonald adds, supported him for years. The suggestion that Cozzens is not only a feeble novelist but also an inept boor cannot be escaped and is clearly not intended to be. Neither can the inference that Cozzens is as much of an anti-Semite, anti-Catholic xenophobe as any of the characters in *By Love Possessed*. One recognizes in this tactic a variant on the ancient *ad hominem* argument of the type: Charlie Chaplin is not a great actor because he did not become an American citizen.

It is not particularly important that using such an argument is dirty pool, but it is important that the instance occurs in what is supposed to be serious criticism. For all most of us know about Cozzens' personal affairs and opinions—which is no more than Macdonald seems to know, the material of a *Time* story—Cozzens may beat his mother, stick pins in babies, and push the old and sick down long flights of stairs. I would hope and trust not, but if my hope is deceived I doubt whether my feelings about his books should be affected. The more one dips into literary biography the more one discovers how much superior writing has been the work of incredible bounders: very few of the great ever deserved to write their masterpieces! And by the same token, some exceedingly pleasant, kindly, moral men have written an astonishing amount of tripe.

Macdonald thinks that it would be good for Cozzens to come and live in New York. Turn about would be very fair play if Cozzens would invite his critic to try living somewhere else, and see how—and by what—people live. But surely no critic really believes that the culture of various back-eddy communities does not produce people like those

in Cozzens' novels. Surely nobody doubts the existence of a
kind of anti-Semitism, generally harmless and often uncon-
scious, among the Arthur Winners of this country. Surely
nobody doubts that there are people, and people who are
utterly in favor of what they proudly call Religious Freedom,
who become nervous about the increasing number of Catholics in their town. The Catholic and the Jew incarnate
change, and change, rather than any inherent characteristic
of the new arrivals, challenges one's position, one's right to
play at being God in the lives of one's dependents and one's
secretary, one's right—why not put it this way?—to be stuffy.
I do not mean this last adjective to condemn such characters
lock, stock, and barrel. A good part of the code by which
men like Arthur Winner live would seem laudable by any
standard: there is nothing wrong that I can see with, for
instance, responsibility and loyalty—both of which mean a
great deal to Winner, and never more than when events
make it difficult for him to know where his responsibilities
and loyalties really lie. But I want to grant Macdonald his
due, and recognize in Cozzens' characters a certain stuffiness. The rest of the point is that this stuffiness—make it even
a Philistine stuffiness, though I doubt that the qualifier is
fully justified—is not the whole story, and that a critical
perspective which sees it loom so large is one which lets it
mask such qualities as Cozzens, as novelist, really possesses.

I do not mean that Cozzens has attained the first rank
of greatness at any point. Frederick Bracher's belief that
four of the novels—the three first mentioned and *Guard
of Honor*—reach real "importance by any set of standards"
is on the hopeful side. By my own standards, which may be
poor things but do incontrovertibly constitute a "set," only
one really measures up: *Guard of Honor*. But if the others
are not absolutely first class, they are still much better than
Macdonald's remarks lead one to think; in all his concern

about values he has missed the very important fact that Cozzens should get credit, to the extent that any individual can ever be credited with anything of the sort, for adding a new dimension to the American novel—or, to avoid having to pause over earlier exceptions like Henry James, with restoring one which has been sorely missing during our lifetimes. This dimension is the vertical one.

Cozzens' principal distinction, which has made him an increasingly better novelist from year to year and in *Guard of Honor* makes him excellent, lies in his having the imagination to place in the very center of a novel a mature man capable of accepting the responsibilities of his age and experience. Taken by and large, the world of the serious American novel is rarely a country for old men. Our fiction has old men in it, of course, in abundance; but they are almost invariably part of some young man's landscape. They are present to be seen but not very often to do the seeing. Lionel Trilling seemed already to be taking himself well off the beaten path when he gave the point of view to a man approaching forty and underlined the fact by referring in his title to Dante's *cammin*. Typical heroes of today are Holden Caulfield, Augie March, and the Invisible Man, just as yesterday they were Eugene Gant, Lieutenant Henry, and Jay Gatsby. It is a fact that the preponderant number of American novels are so exclusively about the young in one another's arms that the individual over thirty-five seems to share with Maupassant's virtuous woman the dubious distinction of having no story worth telling.

Let us not disrupt the folklore of criticism: of course every novel is an adventure in separating the apparent from the real, an account of an education, of an initiation. But one would assume, from a random reading of our novels in just about any year, that initiation and education are early finished, that before middle life the difference between apparent and real is easily distinguished, that education stops well on the hither side of the grave.

Reasons are plentiful why such should be the case. A novelist is limited to writing about human situations into which he has some kind of insight, and insights come hard to the young, simply because the experience to suggest them is not available. A remarkable number of our novels are the work of very young people, to whom some areas are closed by virtue of their youth itself. For example, there is the matter of characters who practice the professions. I have no idea what the statistics on the total output of American fiction writers would show and not much faith in the significance the figures would have if we could get them, but my impression is that most of the novels which have left the deepest mark in recent years have not entrusted the point of view to a character who is engaged in a profession at all, let alone one who is so deeply engaged in his profession that it affects his way of seeing the world around him. The ordinary novelist just does not know enough of what goes on inside a professional man to make such a thing possible. With the exception of teaching, because teaching English is believed by some to provide a way "to earn a living and still have time to write," no profession is open to the man committed to writing fiction. The time when the future professional man is working through his advanced study and internship (whatever form this apprentice period takes) is precisely the time which the writer cannot afford to give up to something other than writing.

Here nothing is at fault but a whole economy of literature which forces a special condition of life on the young writer. He is already buried under commitments anyhow: a wife, school-bills, children, the whole cost exacted from him for being a member of society. These already put him in a position where the risk of writing a bad book involves too many besides himself. A profession would be an additional and even more worrisome commitment, because it would not only add worry but also compete for a major share of the practitioner's attention. True, a man can practice medicine in Paterson, New Jersey, or be an insurance executive in Hartford and still be a serious poet. We honor Dr. Williams and the memory of the late Wallace Stevens. But the pattern is rare, even among poets—and who can say that the conditions of novelist and poet, in this respect, are equivalent? By and large, a commitment to writing fiction and one to a profession exclude each other.

Or put it that writing fiction is itself a profession and does not permit the simultaneous practice of another. Either way, the novelist is automatically debarred from firsthand experience in one great area of our life. For if there is one trait which the world agrees is typically American it is our immense capacity for losing ourselves in our daily business. We are the most dedicated shoptalkers the world has ever known, because we live our shop. Even our national health is menaced, according to report, by our inability to leave affairs behind at the end of the working day. Satire has not cured us: we are still the children of George F. Babbitt, Sam Dodsworth, and the late George Apley. Putting a local twist on the Existentialist tag, we *are* what we *do*. And our understanding of the world, as we mature, is shaped by our professions.

Cozzens' evident ability to understand characters as being molded by profession, and to see the world as such characters see it, is just about unique in American writing. His interest in lawyers has been disparaged as being shallow—and it must be admitted that his lawyers tend to see the law not as a dynamic structure but as a static mechanism for the defense of the status quo. It is curious that one does not hear the same comment on the ministry as represented in *Men and*

Brethren. Such a criticism should not be waved aside, but
it does not say much: these professionals merely share the
common purview of the places they live in—which we may
keep on calling the back-eddy communities. And it remains
true in any case that no one else writing in America, not
even Faulkner, sees into the professions so well. Gavin
Stevens is a lawyer, but it would be very hard to affirm that
he interprets experience according to his training or that
he would behave much differently if he were not a lawyer.
Nothing brings home more firmly than this consideration the
truth that Faulkner's characters are *born* what they are. In
contrast, characters like Arthur Winner, and Judge Ross
of *Guard of Honor,* and even Dr. Bull of *The Last Adam,*
are the product of a half-century of being shaped by what
they have done.

There would seem to be a very visible connection
between the presence in Cozzens' novels of such professional
characters, these older and more experienced men, and his
deep interest in the kind of community he so often writes
about. Such communities are where such men are to be
found most easily, and where they stand out the best. The
back-eddy places are no country for young men; one of
the troubles with these communities is that the most distinguished young are almost inevitably drawn away. Their
talent is worth more elsewhere and back home is, by
definition, where the young "get ahead" least rapidly. Once
they went to the big cities, and indeed they still may; but
now they may also go to the "new areas," all the scientific
and industrial Oak Ridges that spread across the country.
Those who remain at home are likely to be the conservatively
bent (see *The Just and the Unjust*), who are destined to be
as much like their fathers and their grandfathers as they can.
Consequently it is implicit in his whole attitude toward
humanity that Cozzens should have been more attentive

than the common run of novelist to mature and experienced characters. And thus, from his interest in the small-town cultures comes his special excellence and what I am calling the vertical dimension in his fiction. It is what permits him to exploit characters like Judge Ross. Judge Ross is not himself a small-town type, but the small town, even so, is the school where one learns best about such men.

Just to see the world through the eyes of an older man opens a fresh set of perspectives, and these perspectives function in *By Love Possessed*—whatever the book's other defects—as much as they do in *Guard of Honor*. Arthur Winner wears no eagles, but he has a colonel's age and knowledge of life, and a colonel's decisions to make— decisions which have to be made in full awareness of how many lives will be affected besides his own. In many ways, Judge Ross, turned colonel for the duration, is Arthur Winner, Jr., in a uniform. This fact makes *Guard of Honor* a rather special War Novel.

As we got used to it in the years after World War I, this kind of novel was a bit like Kafka's *The Castle*. There are these poor chaps slopping through sticky French mud, sleeping like cattle, perhaps waiting to die. Way off somewhere else is the Command, whence come orders over a one-way line. The circumstances permit the hero to conceive of himself only as victim. Rank, as he knows it, is represented by the shavetail, whom it would be good to shoot in the back. War and the army are the same thing; both are evil; in both the individual is submerged and his personality disintegrated. Drawling lads from Arizona are pushed together with Yankees from Maine, second-generation Italians from San Francisco, Jews (either very sensitive types or else natural comedians) from New York, and somebody or other with a Brooklyn accent. From the first something decreed that this novel should present the melting pot, the composite, gathered from the hillside and called in from the glen: representative America. The good old, and eventually tiresome, formula (it got picked up again after World War II) put the experience of war itself in the center, and drawn in were all these types because while the experience of the war was the same for everybody your way of living through it was individual, representative of something smaller than the complete whole. Always the point of view is the private's, and always his eye looks out along the horizontal plane: when he looks upward nothing he sees is real and when he looks down there is nothing below him.

What the War Novel needed was a good colonel. Norman Ross is not yet a tattered coat upon a stick, but he has been around a while and the material is by no means new: with his blood pressure and his quick fatigues and his worries about his bombardier son, he knows himself for an old man. Like most of the central characters in Cozzens' later books he lives in a sort of quiet and entirely unspectacular desperation. His war is not, as the war was for people in the old War Novel, a vast cosmic imposition or the conspiracy of heaven to crush the individual. It is one of the many things that can happen to a man; it has, though he makes little of the fact, happened to him before—one of the recurrent and therefore interesting forms of human destiny. To the authority of his rank he adds the authority of his ordered, legal mind and of his ordered life.

The Colonel's presence is the making of *Guard of Honor* as novel, because it makes available dimensions which (so far as I can remember at least) have not previously been exploited. The standard formula brought together, in some kind of military unit or other, men of the same rank and the same age; each might see what happened through his own personality, but otherwise what one saw was just about what the next did, because that is what war is. Getting Ross into the novel meant not only that all the behavior of all the people in the piece can be seen from a colonel's vantage—colonels do see more than privates do—but that what he sees is automatically evaluated against the norms which grow out of a mature and intelligent man's experience of life. Entrusting him with the point of view through much of the action was a happy strategy.

So also was not entrusting him with the point of view throughout. Things look different to Captain Nathaniel Hicks because he is younger and his emotions are involved in a different way. Despite his having the rapid comprehension of the trained journalist—here as elsewhere Cozzens defines characters by their professions—Hicks is never in position to get the panoramic view. But he can often be where Ross cannot: while the Colonel watches the parachute-drop from the reviewing stand and is too remote to see what is going on, Hicks, on the lumber pile, is so close to the action that he thinks he may be hit by the falling paratroopers. Each of them has a different angle on General Bus Beal, on Lieutenant Turck, W.A.C., on T/5 Mortimer McIntyre; Hicks is one of several victims of the stupidity of Colonel Mowbray, whereas to Colonel Ross Mowbray's professional fecklessness is a menace of an entirely different kind—it may ruin the usefulness, to the Army Air Force, of General Beal. Hicks and Ross each has his angle on the other principal characters and as in navigation the intersection of two ranges fixes a position, so in the novel each character is located and charted, his role defined with respect to that of the others, by manipulation of the point of view.

But Ross is something more than a technical device. Part of his role is to represent one end of a scale of human values, the other end of which is represented by the irresponsible flyboy Lieutenant-Colonel Benny Carricker. To develop from a good combat commander of combat fliers into the kind of operational commander who can take over the Air Force for the Pacific showdown, General Beal has to grow up and grow up fast. He must, in other words, become less like Carricker and more like Ross. As in all of Cozzens' later novels, the theme of growing up is entirely central. And here again the novel would not exist without Ross. He may not be an entirely convincing character at every point. There are times when he seems too lucid, too quick of understanding, too ready with the right word, too detached. No doubt he is. But everything is relative—and just imagine what the difference would be if he were replaced in *Guard of Honor* by the other colonel of whom we get a close-up in recent fiction.

I take it that this other one, Cantwell in *Across the River and Into the Trees*, is a military version of Hemingway's favorite character, the Old Champ. As virtually everyone who has written about Hemingway has remarked, an old champ is a man who has been hit in the head a lot. But minor cerebral hemorrhages hardly suffice to explain the Colonel's conduct. Take for example the incident where two sailors are attracted to his mistress, the Contessa Renata, beautiful as a fawn and under twenty, while she is walking beside the plus-fifty-year-old Colonel.

There being no one around, Cantwell is in no position to settle matters with a show of rank. Bad heart or no bad heart, he sails in with his fists:

But he hit him with a left from nowhere and hit him three times as he started to go.

The other one, the first whistler, had closed fast and well, for a man who had been drinking, and the Colonel gave him the elbow in the mouth and then, under the light, had a good right hand shot at him. When it was in, he glanced at the other whistler and saw that was okay.

Then he threw a left hook. Then he put the right way into

the body, coming up. He threw another left hook and then turned away and walked toward the girl because he did not want to hear the head hit the pavement.

The loving attention to detail which always marks Hemingway's descriptions of violence is characteristically present. The "left hooks" which are "thrown," the driving right to the body which pushes the entrails out of position and upward, the neatly placed elbow in the mouth (dirty fighting of course but usefully practiced by professionals) transfer the whole scene from the back streets of Venice to Madison Square Garden or at least Stillman's Gym. Like every Hemingway hero, Cantwell knows his stuff and is proficient in technique, just as he is also an excellent shot, Santiago a knowing swordfisherman, Nick Adams a skilled camper. The only trouble with the passage is that one can't believe it.

Field officers of the United States Army are not supposed to be mental giants, but they are hardly likely to attain their rank without showing somewhere along the way at least a modicum of judgment. They are required to estimate situations—as the manuals put it—and as an estimator of situations Cantwell here hits an all-time low. As a man of fifty with heart disease, so full of nitroglycerine that it is a wonder he does not blow up, the best he should hope for is to get his ears pinned well back. At fifty a man has no reflexes; they are not merely out of tune, they are gone. Nor does he have any timing. Nor, consequently, can he punch. The squalid truth is that those left hooks would not break Cantwell's way out of a paper bag. Against two opponents, younger than he and in better condition, he would surely get whipped. A more likely outcome would be sudden death.

But just suppose that one of these younger men, instead of accepting the fight and "closing in well," had grabbed Cantwell's arms long enough for the other to strip him of his belt and a few strategic buttons and then simply walked away! One can imagine a sick old man, even though Cantwell has up to now shown no desire at all to hasten the processes of nature, piling angrily into a fight at the risk of his life, but it is a lot harder to imagine a colonel (in this case one who has lately been a brigadier general) accepting the risk of humiliation in the presence of the youthful beauty whom he loves.

It is easier to imagine Colonel Cantwell's taking Contessa Renata firmly by a beautiful arm and hurrying her away from the whistling wolves, outraged and ashamed, and afterward lapsing into a fantasy in which he is young and well, with reflexes in tune, speed in his feet, and a punch in each fist, and ready to fight an imaginative rematch in which everything came out to his satisfaction. But I have to imagine him, also, snapping out of his fantasy after a gratifying moment, distinguishing it from reality, and facing the facts of being fifty and slow and minus his reflexes.

At this juncture it is absolutely impossible not to revert to Colonel Ross. He has Cantwell's rank and, in the form of age and high blood pressure, some of his disabilities. But he also has what Cantwell sometimes lacks, the ability to know when he is dreaming and when he is awake. Faced with the job of helping Bus Beal and keeping Benny Carricker in line, Cantwell would be at a considerable disadvantage: he has never really convinced himself that he is maturer than Carricker. His own world is pretty much the world of the flyboy. The man who wants to keep Bus Beal in touch with reality had better be in rather close touch with reality himself.

Hemingway's two attempts to write stories about old men have hardly come up to his best work. *Across the River* is what a book with Cantwell for a hero would have to be, a compilation of adolescent wish-fulfilments; *The Old Man and the Sea* is an allegory demonstrating, simultaneously, first that old age hath yet its honor and its toil, and second that an old man may not be so old after all. But where would any old men, living the lives of old men, find their way into his world? With the exception of the stories about Nick Adams he always wrote the stories of men away from home. They turn up in Spain, Italy, France, the Caribbean, the snowy slopes of Kilimanjaro—places where the life of an older American is unlikely to have much inherent meaning. For such D.P.'s age is nothing more than the absence of youth. For novelists wanting to write about characters who are beyond the prime of life, the advantage of seeing those characters in surroundings where years do not inhibit their functioning should be obvious. And the later novels of Cozzens are available to show that the advantage can be taken.

Obviously this special excellence leads Cozzens into equally special dangers. The characters he prefers are likely to belong to the well-off middle class, or else to be firmly allied to it. Even in the present moment of "consolidation" and conformity, real or alleged, fiction is likely to treat such people without sympathy. They doubt the value of social change, not so much from principle as because they have reached an age where adjusting to change of any sort is no longer easy. Such dispositions are unheroic to say the least; sclerosis is not a source of admirable motives; their will to endure becomes indistinguishable from a mere wanting to hang on. Attempts to make the reader love them will not often succeed.

I suspect that here we are close to having the reason why *Guard of Honor* is so toweringly superior to *By Love Possessed*. *Guard of Honor* is not a book about Norman Ross as the later one is about Arthur Winner. We are not expected to contemplate Ross for his own sake, and the outcome of the story is not identical with the final stage of his fortunes. He is important in the novel, but important in relation to what happens to all the people at the air installation called AFORAD and, like the other people in the story, with what happens to AFORAD itself and ultimately to the progress of a war. On the other hand, Winner is close to being the total subject of *By Love Possessed,* an extremely difficult subject as subjects for novels go. For such a novel to succeed the tone would have to be exactly right.

And the tone of *By Love Possessed* is wrong. The world Winner lives in is somehow mean. His family relationships, his essay in adultery, his dealings with the associate he has meaninglessly cuckolded, his problem of whether or not to reveal Noah Tuttle's rascality add up to very little in the way of moral stature. Such a man's life can be a minor-key tragedy. In the kind of community Cozzens knows so well and that Winner is a part of, some men ripen, others go directly from greenness to decay, but most of them merely wither and grow small. Most of us, having some knowledge of the quality of life in such a community, would have some sympathy for Arthur Winner, if we were permitted to.

But a pressure is on the reader always to share Winner's personal dispositions. The choice of an adjective in one place implies that if something strikes Winner in such and such a way it will surely strike you so, too; the choice of a verb somewhere else assumes our participation in the action. To give a harmless example, there is a passage where Arthur Winner walks past the abandoned ark where Noah Tuttle used to live and which no one now wants to occupy; he feels a touch of sadness because people do not want to inhabit such monstrosities any more. From Winner this is typical and the emotion is entirely in character; for the reader, unless he is a Winner himself, such a feeling would be the emptiest sentimentality—and there is not enough room left open between character and reader for the two to have separate and appropriate emotions.

It would help, of course, if one were permitted to see what happens in *By Love Possessed*, at least from time to time, through eyes other than those of its central figure. It would do no harm if, occasionally, we could see him as his fellow-citizens saw him. Better still if, once or twice, we could see him as he looked to a complete outsider, who would see him as the old pre-Jamesian novel used to see its characters, as an individual surrounded by his environment. But we do not have such opportunities and, accordingly, the distance—which is essentially a matter of tone—being all off, the reader feels a constant effort to involve him, to get him to identify himself with Arthur Winner, which amounts to a kind of falsification.

In their first fine, careless rapture, the reviewers who went overboard for *By Love Possessed* agreed in picturing a Cozzens who, from very unimpressive beginnings in books like *Confusion* (1924) and *Michael Scarlett* (1925), had gradually, painfully worked his way through exercise and experiment — S.S. *"San Pedro"* (1931) and *Castaway* (1934) —toward mastery of his craft: *Men and Brethren* (1936), *The Just and the Unjust* (1943), *Guard of Honor* (1948), on to an apotheosis in *By Love Possessed*. Even the thoughtful Frederick Bracher, though less inclined to forget that the climb to the heights was interrupted by books like *The Last Adam* (1933) and *Ask Me Tomorrow* (1940), and aware of certain imperfections in *By Love Possessed*, tends to take the same view. To the extent that critics like Macdonald correct it by insisting that the last-named novel is something of a botched job, and after *Guard of Honor* may be even tawdry, they have been useful, timely, and right. Cozzens' climb has not been steady and there is a sharp down-bend after the top of the curve.

But the nature of Cozzens' descent cannot be particularly apparent to a critic who does not distinguish between the personal defects of the character Arthur Winner and the views, attitudes, and dispositions which are characteristic of anyone who is condemned—or privileged—to lead the kind of American life Winner leads. As a revelation of the precise content of one kind of life in America *By Love Possessed*, with all its faults, is a much better book than those who do not know the circumstances of that kind of life would think. Beyond the Hudson rise the Palisades, which would seem to block the perspective of some three thousand miles of country where the culture is, to say a part of the truth, not all of a piece. And to the south and north men are not always and everywhere entirely like each other, either.

5

Edna St. Vincent Millay:
Little Girl Lost

WHEN Edna St. Vincent Millay died—in October, 1950, alone in her house near Austerlitz, New York—all the obituaries could recall of her poetry was the stuff from *A Few Figs from Thistles.* Her candle had burned at both ends; she had built her shining palace on the sand; her true love had been false; they had been riding back and forth all night on the ferry. And in spite of all Edmund Wilson could do in his remarkable "Memoir," and all that Vincent Sheean could do in his book, and with the *Collected Poems* at hand for anyone who wants to read, and such of her letters as got included in the published correspondence, she will undoubtedly go down in history as the little country girl who came to the big city and wrote brightly defiant poems which spoke of love in unconventional circumstances. Possibly it is better for her to be remembered as the muse of MacDougal Street than not at all, but she deserved to be remembered better, or if not better at least more accurately. Her *Figs* were exceptional and not particularly characteristic, and the apparently permanent public image of her as a college girl lately escaped from Vassar and dedicated to kicking coltishly over all sorts of traces simply dismisses the life work of a serious and highly conservative poet in favor of a half-dozen impertinent jingles. But to know this it is necessary to know the rest of her poetry and something about her life.

She was born in Rockland, Maine, but grew up in Camden, which is some eight miles up Penobscot Bay from Rockland and an entirely different kind of town. Rockland is commercial, and ugly; Camden was and is a beautiful place. Superficially it has not changed greatly since the 1890's; only the special inner quality of the life there has deteriorated. The town is built around a harbor, into the head of which drops a small river that drains a lake four miles back behind the hills. In front is the Bay with its islands—Isleboro up to the left, the Foxes down the Bay to the right, Isle au Haut, Swan's Island, Deer Isle and Blue Hill off beyond to the east; and on clear days there is Mount Desert Island with Cadillac Mountain looming up on the horizon beyond Frenchman's Bay. Behind the town, rising almost out of the water, are Mount Battie, Mount Megunticook, and a third sharp hill which must be on the map but whose name nobody ever seems to know. Highway Number 1 runs through Main Street, and its doing so is what has changed the quality of the life.

So long as there was no bridge over the Kennebec River at Bath, Camden was not on a main thoroughfare. The steam ferry which served those bound farther eastward discouraged all but the hardiest tourist, and only when the bridge was finally in place, in the late twenties, did the town follow the rest of New England in making the accommodation of anonymous nomads its principal business. Until then its summer population was stable: the same people came summer after summer and they came to stay the summer out, from just before the Fourth of July until just after Labor Day, in their own houses for the most part. These people considered themselves part of the town and were recognized as such; their proxies spoke in town meeting, and since their taxes could be counted on in the yearly budget, what they asked for they generally got. And around this nucleus of property owners gathered the "summer boarders" who did not own their own places but like the others came regularly and came to stay all summer. These part-time residents constituted—everything is relative—a more or less cultivated squirearchy who took their share of responsibilities.

Well they might. The Bay, unless one tries to swim in it, is lovely. The harbor was just right for their launches and yachts. The land they built on—modest places as rich men's homes went, but impressive by local standards—commanded immensely satisfactory seascapes (and, being ledge, became taxable as it would never otherwise have been). They financed such things as the town library, the YMCA, and the summer baseball team.

But after Labor Day everything settled rapidly down. The steamer from Boston went on reduced schedule for a few weeks, then stopped entirely for the winter. The Maine Central cut the number of trains into Rockland and took off the sleepers from Washington and New York. Big houses were boarded up, and the caretakers moved into other jobs for the winter. The little textile mills up river from the center could take on a few experienced hands; there was a certain amount of boat repair and even building; the lime quarries just over the line in Rockport absorbed a few; some went to lobstering until it got too cold. In general, Camden banked its houses with brush and nailed itself down for the winter.

Culturally the town was now on its own. The Protestant ministry was educated. (Catholicism moved out for the winter when the summer residents took their house servants back to the cities.) The lawyers were mostly men who had "read" in other men's offices, but who—as a group—had kept the habit of reading; schoolteachers, who were likely to be local people, were as highly respected as they were low paid. These were the leaders of a place which, from September through June, was self-contained to an extent today incredible.

An afternoon spent going through the files of the Camden *Herald* for the year 1909—which was the year of Edna Millay's graduation from high school—leaves the impression that this self-containment was complete: little if any national or state news, complete indifference to international affairs. Camden had voted solidly for Taft the year before, but was far more interested by issues to come up in town meeting. What the *Herald's* readers wanted was local news and, surprisingly, there was enough to fill each weekly issue.

Social life was clearly the responsibility of the churches, Baptist, Methodist, Congregational, Episcopalian; of the flourishing fraternal orders, of the Grange. Except for one importation, a prestidigitator brought in by a "Lodge," all entertainment was by local talent. Clubs and "circles" proliferated and met regularly. Such music as there was came in the form of concerts in the churches, arranged by choir directors who were more familiar, it would appear, with the compositions of the late Dudley Buck than with those of Bach or Beethoven. It all sounds more culturally active than the present Camden; certainly the local life required local participation, long since replaced by passivity at the movie or before the television. It also sounds morally supervised, conservative, stodgy, and dull.

Morals were a community concern, since everyone knew his neighbor's business. They were also strict: especially in sex matters Camden's disposition was severely Calvinist. But the point should not be exaggerated; if Calvinism was absolute in theory, in practice considerable indulgence was accorded the sexual impetuosities of the young. There is now no way to verify the statement of one of the town's ministers that half the marriages he performed were, to use his word, "involuntary," but witnesses still live who heard him say so. The more sporting young men, who spent their Saturday evenings in the fleshpots of Rockland—which had saloons and even a cat house on Crockett's Point—were deplored by many but by no means universally condemned. Later, when Camden read Edna Millay's poetry and heard rumors of experimental ménages, what produced shock was probably much less the rumored activity than the poetry that, presumably, was written about it, and less the poetry than the fact that the poetry had been written. The subject just did not fall within the canon of locally accepted *topoi*.

In many ways, Camden was a good place to grow up. There were few of the problems of adjustment which confront children in more complex communities. The recurrent presence of the summer squirearchy gave local society a structure of a sort; you knew who you were, summer or native, and your status was solid. If you were native, there was no point in trying to be anything else; and where none of your kind had money, it was unimportant whether you had a little less or a little more. But on the other hand, if eventually you abandoned that life for another one, the chances were that you would have to do a great deal of adjusting, because you discovered your economic and cultural deficiencies all at once, at an age when adjustment is far from automatic.

Except for a brief stay in Massachusetts, Edna Millay was brought up in Camden by her mother, Cora, who was by all accounts a remarkable woman. The home was a broken one: Cora and her three girls had stayed on in Camden when the father had picked up and moved inland from the coast. Money was short and the town knew that the Millays were hard up, but Cora managed. She was a good practical nurse, and when no one needed care she had other resources—such as peddling "rats" and "switches" to the back-country farmers' women, false hair being then considered elegant. Obviously the Millays had no easy go of it, but Camden considered the family to be a happy one. Edna Millay's high-school teachers thought that she was brighter than most, and one of them kept her verse translations of Virgil for years. She won a prize, in her last year, for a poem.

This distinction was greater than it may seem, for writing poetry was an esteemed activity, and of poetesses, especially, there were God's plenty. Penobscot Bay has always had its competent poets, some native to the ground like Wilbert Snow and Harold Vinal, others from "outside" like James Agee and Daniel G. Hoffman. But the indigenous muse spoke through others who were obscurer, and inglorious though certainly not mute. There were women in and around Camden who could be moved to verse at what was quite clearly very brief notice indeed. The turn of a season, a red leaf, a violet, a death or a birth, less often a marriage, the return of a relative from away, or an anniversary could set them off. The "poetry corners" of the *Herald,* and of the Rockland *Courier-Gazette,* were catholically hospitable. Some of these women, like Anna Coughlin of Rockland and Martha W. Hanley of Warren, managed words with recognizable skill, but such gifts were something extra and by no means requisite. (A brief study of the accepted rhymes provides a remarkable introduction to the phonetic vagaries of Down-East speech.) Most essential was to be moved by the right inspirations, the accepted and recognized ones. Everybody knew what poetry should be about.

Among those who could, when the mood was on her, take pen in hand was Cora Millay. One of her productions, a threnody, appears in the *Herald* of 1909. True, even the

best disposed of critics could not hold forth at great length
on what merits the poem has, and among these merits origi-
nality surely would not figure. But this fact is of small importance. What counts is that Edna Millay, who probably never
saw an original painting of any quality, or heard serious
music professionally performed, until she was an adult, grew
from childhood in an atmosphere and in a home where it
was natural for women to write verse. The fact is of consequence.

But not immediately: she finished high school and went
to work in Job Montgomery's law office, where but for a bit
of luck she might have stayed. There was no money to send
her to college. She was still working there in 1912, when
some of the summer women heard that she had written
some poetry, and then heard the poetry. They felt that she
should go to college, and later that year she left Camden;
there were a few months in New York, at Barnard, and then
the four years at Vassar. By the time she was graduated
(1917) she had written enough for a small book. She was,
in other words, beginning to keep her promise. She was—it
should be added—just four months short of being twenty-
five.

To judge by *Renascence* she was young for her age. How
much it had meant to her to get out of Camden and open up
her life is a great deal more visible in her correspondence
than in these early poems—some of which, of course, were
written before she had left home at all. The themes are
conventional: death and rebirth, nature, love, disappointment in love, the experience of sorrow and bereavement.
All of these, clearly, had been available to the inhabitants
of the shore towns of Maine, and to poets writing in papers
like the *Herald*. More personal is the device, which would
later become her badge, of combining a depressed mood,
flippant words, and a lilting rhythm:

> Death, I say, my heart is bowed,
>   Unto thine,—O mother!
> This red gown will make a shroud
>   Good as any other.

In a few years she will exploit this combination, perhaps beyond reason; it will become part of her recognizable "manner"—suffering suggested by the intentional irony created by the contrast between content and form:

> After all, my erstwhile dear,
>   My no longer cherished,
> Need we say it was not love,
>   Just because it perished?

The tone is not unlike Dorothy Parker's more or less contemporaneous one, although not so harsh, bitter, and self-lacerating or self-mocking. But it is only incidental in this first collection: the general impression one gets from it today is timidity. Some of the freshness and delicacy its early readers recognized still remains, but one is rather more aware of a singular unadventurousness. The forms, well mastered though they are, are the easy nineteenth-century ones. She appears to want words to do no more than words are called upon to do every day; there is no strain upon her resources. She does not see very much of the exterior world, nor does she see very precisely. Concrete detail is very largely absent. Such metaphors as she uses are subdued and most often operate to express feeling rather than to interpret it.

The quality of the feeling is adolescent. When she is happy she is determined to be the gladdest toucher and non-picker of flowers under the sun, who cannot hold the lovely world close enough. Love goes off and leaves her and life goes on forever like the gnawing of a mouse. God is a kindly parent who is not angry at his children who commit suicide but gives them no further job to do. In general she is wide-eyed and somewhat breathless and a trifle girlish, not to say elaborately innocent. This was poetry for the more sophisticated and literate ladies' clubs.

Next (1920) came the *Figs from Thistles* collection: the candle and the house on the sand, the ferry and life on MacDougal Street. Rereading these poems on the occasion of her death set her generation off on a jag of reminiscence rather like the one earlier churned up by the death of Scott Fitzgerald. One had been young and gay and indisposed to give much of a damn about anything at all, had done what one liked and defied Mrs. Grundy. Edna Millay's hedonism had been the Voice of an Age. The obituaries made much of the fact that when her body was found, in the house near Austerlitz, a bottle of wine and a wineglass were near by. None, so far as I know, actually referred to her death as the end of a "priestess of revolt," but the ironic implication was everywhere.

Priestess of revolt indeed! In this second phase of her development she was doing exactly what she had done in the first: conforming to the going taste, accepting the *topoi* in vogue. Just as in *Renascence* she had orchestrated the themes dear to the lady poets of Penobscot Bay, so now she was again proving how sensitive she was to what was in the air around her. The pity is that she did it so well. The image she left of herself, her public *persona,* is hard to eradicate and is one of a twenty-year-old. The recurrent error which creeps into accounts of American writing in the twenties and makes it sound as if she came bursting out of Vassar like the Young Monk from Siberia has a certain justification: women usually emerge from college as they reach their majority, and *Figs* makes Edna Millay sound as if she had just reached hers or were just about to. She was, in cold fact, twenty-eight. The girls of her class in the Camden High School were starting their second, or even third, round of babies; some of them—diets were bad during the war—had lost their teeth, gained weight, had time to realize that their husbands would do little better by them financially than they were doing right then and that they faced lives of routine housework or small jobs. Their classmate was writing about candles when they had reason to consider themselves on the threshold of middle age. To be entirely blunt about it, she was taking her own time about growing up. Crossing the cultural gulf which separated life in a town where folkways and mores were still those of the preceding century from life where it was the fashion not to want to settle down—after war which had in some ways been a great vacation—had delayed her arrival at emotional and poetic maturity. She was still, at twenty-eight, years away from work like *Conversation at Midnight,* and long before she was ready to write anything of that quality, her reputation had crystallized indestructibly.

This fact, among others, explains the success of the late Samuel Hoffenstein's little parody:

> I want to drown in good-salt water,
> I want my body to bump the pier;
> Neptune is calling his wayward daughter,
> Saying, "Edna, come over here!"

In factual truth, Edna Millay wrote very little of the fishtrap and seaweed poetry which has been a standard product of the Down-East muse. And much of what she did write of it is superior of its kind: see "Low Tide." But she did have, especially in the earlier years, some tendency to combine the inspiration of the clamflat with the mood expressed by the girlish gasp:

> I would be happy who have been happy
> All day long on the coast of Maine...

And this, for Hoffenstein's purposes, was all it took.

Actually, her feeling for her native soil was very real and strong, but one sees this better, perhaps, in her prose. In her introduction to the translation of Baudelaire which she did with George Dillon she discusses the difficulties the translator finds in the fact that certain emotions are better expressed in French than in the English semi-equivalents. Her example is the homely one: driving between Waldoboro and Warren on the way to Camden, after an absence, your car noses over the crest of a rise and there suddenly in front of you are the hills; you see them now not across water but land, but there they are (as she does *not* say), the "three long mountains and a wood." And the phrase that comes to you first is the French one: "C'est mon pays." She was one of the few latter-day New England poets who ever managed to speak of their region without phoniness or vulgarity.

Such an accomplishment is no mean one. It was, for example, beyond the reach of Robert Frost. This is not an opportune moment to say so, when adulation of Frost is almost universal, but there are places in his work where he creates a cracker-barrel New Hampshire, inhabited by farmers more laconic, and wiser in their simplicity, than men ever are, anywhere. This is the Frost who uses their laconism (as Marcus Cunliffe has remarked) to evade the problem of expressing a complete emotion fully. This is the California native who from time to time (not always and not in his best work) makes New Hampshire a home for values elsewhere forgotten, in a way which might surprise even the oldest residents: who makes a symbol for integrity of a home-hewn ax-helve, an artifact most New Hampshire people have always bought at hardware stores and use awkwardly, if ever; who wrote "New Hampshire" and "Brown's Descent." This Frost is the one who has retreated backward over the culture-lag and swallows hard at his Adam's apple to indi-

cate emotion, and salts his wisdom to taste—and takes refuge
in a folksiness which may not be phony but is indeed vulgar.
If Frost falls into such a trap, the trap must be a real one.

Edna Millay avoided it. In spite of what Hoffenstein did
to her—and his parody is an eloquent criticism of her earlier
work—she managed to take joy in her region without falsi-
fying her relation to it. In her later poetry it stands as the
place where she was once happier and more secure than
she has been since, where the native going back can feel
that his roots here go deep as the roots of the trees, where
it is good to be, but where, even so, one does not stay.

But this mood *was* a late one. Earlier she was in fact
vulnerable. She had the old and possibly naïve notion that
lyric was song, and there were times when she was like a
tenor trying to tear the heart out of his audience anent some
subject which he does not feel very deeply himself. At such
moments she is—according to how well one likes her work—
either adopting a *persona* or merely posing. And laying herself open to Hoffenstein's "I speak the speech of the wild
sardine."

The devil-may-care, bohemian, hedonist *persona* did not
last long. And apart from it there is astonishingly little sign
of anything like revolt in her work. She returned, shortly,
to the tone of the wonder-smitten and often hurt little girl.
Life was rough (how rough she had perhaps not discovered
when she first started to say so) and one needs more cour-
age than one has; death is not good nor does he go back
docilely to his kennel; love is good but brings disappointment; the world is lovely, but loveliness is not particularly
helpful; the human race can be abominable, but is not always
so; and God has some relation to all this but the relation is
always vague—her theology is always somewhat vaporous,
even though, such as it is, it does save her from ever sound-
ing like Housman. It was from this *persona,* rather than

the hedonist one, that she took longest to extricate herself. She took so long, in fact, that well before she had reached the fulness of *Mine the Harvest* and the later sonnets, the kind of poetry she wrote was out of fashion.

She was, it is appropriate to remember, a poet of experience; the experience was personal and its range was small. It had to be experience she had known herself, because it was experience such as everyone without exclusion has had —so familiar, it may be reiterated, that very few of her subjects had not been treated by her elders along Penobscot Bay. (We are talking here of kind and not of quality.) She exploited and re-exploited it copiously, intending, always, a sharper definition of feeling and very little more. This in an age of Eliot and Auden, of William C. Williams, of Wallace Stevens, of Pound!

Besides which, when every other poet was consumed by the need of discovering new resources, she remained thoroughly untempted by experiment. Her vocabulary stayed surprisingly small, her respect for established syntax absolute; and she never seems to strain against the form, to be limited by it, to be prevented by it from saying what she has to say. "Hard" and obscure poetry became the rule. We preferred what seemed new, strange, and in need of interpretation—therefore interesting. For Edna Millay a lapse was not a tumble into complete obscurity of language, but a descent into ordinary prose:

> ... But the rain
> Is full of ghosts tonight, that tap and sigh
> Upon the glass, and listen for reply ...

One could claim for her that she had mastered the sonnet as no one else since Elizabeth Barrett. But the age demanded not Mrs. Browning but her husband, and above them both preferred Gerard Manley Hopkins.

To say it all at once, she was delayed in her development by the fact that she grew up in one kind of American culture and moved to another, and the delay resulted in one of those critical distortions which are so common. If she was a *révoltée* she was one only for a moment; for the rest of her life, before and after, she was quite the opposite. If she was the sweet singer of the Village, and Provincetown and the Lost Generation, she was more, also—how much more it would not be good to ignore.

6

Emily Dickinson: God's Little Girl

FEW FACTS about Emily Dickinson are undisputed. One of these is that, shortly after she had asked T. W. Higginson for his help, she discovered that what she was writing would mean nothing to the contemporary American audience, and thus became an early example of the alienated American poet. Quite possibly her first experiences with editors, and Higginson's own inability to adjust to something new, misled her: her lack of confidence in the public may have been mistaken. Certainly the immediate stir of interest in her poems upon their posthumous publication makes one suspect that she overestimated, perhaps because she was obscurely eager to overestimate, the difficulties of communication. But the fact that imperviousness is rarely universal does not alter the other fact of her feeling that when she spoke few were prepared to listen. She had fallen into that state of mind which magnifies the separation of the "I" from the "They," of the ego from whatever is outside the self and presumably hostile toward it. Or, to use a language which must seem barbarous in the context, she found "inner-directedness" to imply a generous measure of discomfort.

Obviously this subject can be overdone: she was never, in spite of the white dresses and the flitting about behind curtains when visitors called and all the twaddle which has at times been popular about "the nun of Amherst," so completely withdrawn from other people as a dramatic but incompletely informed notion of her would have it. Her letters fill three volumes and many of them went through preliminary drafts. Nor did some literary schizophrenia allow her to correspond in prose while keeping her poetry to herself: she encloses some hundreds of her poems in letters. Nothing in this sounds like a spirit which had turned its face resolutely and absolutely away from the world outside. Painful shyness—even so painful as to justify the adjective pathological—is one thing; utter alienation is quite another. In fact, the more one learns about Emily Dickinson, the saner she sounds, and the harder it is to share the conviction that writing poetry was all that kept her in temper.

But we have been abundantly reminded in recent years by critics intent upon avoiding biographical interpretation and the genetic fallacy that the "I" which speaks in a poem is not necessarily, and perhaps not at all, the "I" bearing the poet's name, which brushes its teeth every morning and evening and carries on all the other commerce of everyday life. Most allegedly personal lyrics, in other words, have something of the dramatic monologue about them. No doubt this concept, too, could bear some close and unsympathetic examination. Useful as it may be, for correcting the abuse of biography, to grant that almost any poet does create some *persona* as he writes, there must surely be degrees of the autonomy of such *personae* from poet to poet, ranging from minor wish-fulfilling corrections of what the poet feels to be his own personality to characters just about as independent as figures in a play. There must also be degrees of awareness, in the poet, of what he is doing. I have no wish to exaggerate the importance of the various *personae* of Emily Dickinson; yet, even so, there is a more audible sound of alienation in some of her poetry than there is in the letters, and in such poems the "I" more firmly distin-

guishes itself from the "They" than was the case in her
actual life.

For example:

> I'm ceded—I've stopped being Their's—
> The name They dropped upon my face
> With water, in the country church
> Is finished using, now,
> And They can put it with my Dolls,
> My childhood, and the string of spools
> I've finished threading—too—
>
> Baptized, before, without the choice,
> But this time, consciously, of Grace—
> Unto supremest name—
> Called to the full—the Crescent dropped—
> Existence's whole arc, filled up,
> With one small Diadem.
>
> My second rank—too small the first—
> Crowned—Crowing—on my Father's breast—
> A half unconscious Queen—
> But this time—Adequate—Erect,
> With Will to choose, or to reject,
> And I choose, just a Crown—

The fact that this, according to Thomas H. Johnson's
variorum edition, is an unfinished "worksheet" draft increases
rather than lessens its interest, because of its evidence that
the subject was one the poet had difficulty in treating or—
more precisely—in treating completely: all nine instances
where a variant or variants presented alternative possibilities to her are in the second half of the poem. Apparently
she felt no ambiguity or ambivalence about the first half.

The opposition of two sacraments, which forms the
poem's structural frame, becomes complex precisely because
of the ambiguity of the second part, beginning with the

eleventh line. Obviously the second sacrament is matrimony, as clearly as the first one is baptism, but as always in her poems, matrimony is an extremely complex state. It is, as Charles R. Anderson is the most recent critic to insist, one of celestial as well as earthly blessedness, combining the connubial bliss which she missed in this life with some supernatural union; her lover may have worn, in her imagination, the features of someone like the Reverend Samuel Wadsworth, but it is never entirely certain that he is not, to some extent, also God. All the talk about "rank," "Crown," and "Diadem," familiar from all her writing about the realization of love, places an emphasis upon heavenly rather than earthly beatitude; in Protestant hymnology such language is connected with salvation. Orthodox theology is irrelevant here, or it would be in order to talk of heresy: matrimony is not requisite for salvation, but baptism is indispensable. Actually she is imagining two states of grace, the first of which is inferior to the second, the second infinitely more valuable because voluntarily assumed and also because it is a fulfilment. In other words, the sacrament which has conferred the new, more satisfactory condition is a *rite de passage*.

Anderson, who has done a remarkable job of learning her language, leaves no doubt as to what she means by "Adequate." She uses it in its etymological sense of being entirely equal to any demand; like the word *perfection*, this one must be defined negatively: no requisite is lacking. As the filled "arc" is to the "Crescent" of existence, so is her present state to her previous, merely baptized, one. Her toys, and those spools hung like beads on a string which in New England took the place of toys, may now be put away. She need no longer play: she is completely and triumphantly adult.

It is doubtful if any habitual reader of Emily Dickin-

son will contest the general tendency of this reading. Too
many others among her poems identify wifehood not only
with the experience of new transcendent joys and unbear-
able but precious bereavements, but also with the ultimate
development of the personality. It may be underlined that
this is *only one* of the manifold meanings of the second
state to her, but *one* of them it seems irrefutably to be.
Perhaps paradoxically, there need be less speculation by
interpreters about this condition than about the first, the
seemingly unambiguous one, which caused her no trouble
to write (see the absence of variants), but which opens
a whole series of questions.

For it states explicitly the fundamental opposition
between "I" and "They." In that first state—which, it should
be remembered, she never escaped save by the function of
her imagination—she does not belong to herself: she is
"Their's," whomever the possessive pronoun may indicate.
Moreover, she is theirs in the sense of a piece of property:
ceded applies to something one may own, and properly
speaking the only human being who can be ceded is a slave.
In the awful, frightening, literal meaning of the expression,
she cannot call her soul her own. The condition of being
"Their's" has prevented her from realizing her own happiness, and we are naturally impelled to try to identify the
reference.

Her father is specifically invoked in association with
the ceremony of inducting the "I" into the first, incomplete
state. And the identification is re-enforced by the choice of
the first verb in the poem, "ceded." In addition to applying
to property rather than to persons, *ceded* is also a legal
word; Edward Dickinson was a lawyer. But it would be a
hideous oversimplification to identify the Non-"I" or even
the Anti-"I" with one person, since the pronoun in the poem
is, after all, plural. And the invocation of the father may be

less significant than it first seems because, in the strict Protestant ceremony where there is no godfather to take the vows for the child, the real father would be the natural choice to hold the infant at the font. And in addition, if Edward was a lawyer, so was Emily's beloved brother Austin. These considerations do not entirely dismiss Edward's candidacy, but they do make it more reasonable to assume that "Their's" could just as well refer to the Dickinson family as a whole and even go beyond the limits of the family to embrace, if not the whole community, those members of it whose lives came into contact with the poet's. If the "I" of the poem is to a certain extent fictive, then why should not the "Their's" involve a fictive entity also?

Only the most literal-minded biographer would take this reading to imply a condemnation of the Dickinson family and their friends. The role of an unmarried daughter of a middle-class family in New England was necessarily a restricted one. The economy of life in a small town, especially, offered few opportunities for self-realization outside the family, and within the family there was no adult status reserved; a daughter could not expect, except in rare instances, to occupy any but a filial role in the eyes of her parents. Such a life was organized as if expressly to make the achievement of complete adulthood difficult if not impossible. She could be expected to have exasperated moments when she would be happy to give them back their name, to keep along with the toys and spools and string which characterized her unproductive condition. It does not seem unreasonable to take this poem as an expression of such a mood.

But meanwhile this urgent desire for adult status, this ardent wish to grow up, which may and probably does include the desire and wish for sexual fulfilment but certainly transcends these if it does not hypostasize them, becomes the more interesting because it can be discussed only as an aspect of Emily Dickinson's ambivalence. For she also slipped easily into the *persona* of a child and seems, often, to have enjoyed it.

Anderson remarks that she played a lifelong game of being a little girl, and certainly there is ample support for this view in the correspondence. Some of her letters, in later life, strike one as outrageously kittenish, until the reader realizes that they are addressed to correspondents who have known her for a time and are used to her mood. Doubtless, also, some of the little-girl tone is put on for an occasion and to please the people to whom she writes, as for example the Norcross cousins. It is also notorious that when she wrote to children she was admirably capable of putting herself on the level of the child. But the persistence of the trait, which, as Anderson remarks, lasted as long as Emily Dickinson lived, suggests that something was going on here besides a game. As has been very frequently remarked, the men to whom she attached herself sentimentally—at whatever distance and whether they were aware of it or not—were all older than she. Wadsworth and Judge Lord were nearer her father's age than her own, and her perception of the difference between lover and surrogate father may not have been particularly acute. From her relationship with B. F. Newton on through her life she revealed a recurrent need to elect mentors. She signed her letters to Higginson, "Your scholar."

The juvenile tone also is audible in many of the poems besides those which were patently written for a juvenile audience. Especially in the early years of her writing she falls into it very easily indeed. Not always, by any means, is the habit detrimental to her poetry: a good bit of what Anderson calls her wit, and George F. Whicher her humor, derives from her ability to see an object as a child would see it, i.e.

as it actually is, unconditioned by all the prejudices and
false qualifications which affect the vision of adults; her
poem about the railroad train, huffing and puffing its meaningless way along the valley, succeeds because she divorces
the silly thing completely from the human and, especially,
economic aspects which largely determine the attitude taken
by adults. And there is sheer delight in her image of herself as God's "little tippler leaning against the sun."

It strikes some readers as less felicitous when she is being
satirical on the subject of the new science:

> Perhaps the "Kingdom of Heaven's" changed—
> I hope the "Children" there
> Won't be "new fashioned" when I come—
> And laugh at me—and stare—
>
> I hope the Father in the skies
> Will lift his little girl—
> Old fashioned—naughty—everything—
> Over the gates of "Pearl."

Here it would seem that a poem which constitutes an
artful attack upon a very serious human enterprise deserved
some ending other than this reversion to the juvenile. To
become, at the end, God's "little girl" implies in a way a
refusal to take full responsibility for the criticism inherent
in the piece. But of course the Calvinist Protestantism in
which her birth had implanted her, with its great emphasis
upon the anthropomorphic Fatherhood of God, its insistence upon becoming as a little child in order to enter into
the Kingdom and of suffering little children, its persistent
placing of the faithful in a filial relationship to the Almighty,
had given her, as it did everyone, an abundant stock of
cliché to juggle. One may, while not caring deeply for the
poem, still feel that in the instance the final girlishness of
mood is not of consequence.

But it keeps turning up—as anyone who reads her through in the Johnson edition knows. And sometimes even in her best work, meaning here by "best" the poems which find their way most often into the anthologies. Here is a striking example:

> Because I could not stop for Death—
> He kindly stopped for me—
> The Carriage held but just ourselves—
> And immortality—

After the manner common to young gentlemen of the time and place, a suitor has come to invite his lady to the ritual of courting, the carriage ride outside the town. And if a lady has suitors she is, by definition, young, a maid, unfulfilled. Her poem which, out of all her work, comes the nearest to expressing a reconciliation with death is thus one in which she accepts him before she has completely grown up.

In both *personae* the poet appears as alienated. There is always the "they" from which she differentiates herself. "They" would do better to have a less repellent religion, just as they would do better (by implication anyhow) not to mess up the landscape with their railroad, or not to practice a science which reveals the indifference of the physical universe. In what she wrote for children, in prose and verse, the tone insists: *we* know and understand even if *they* don't. Childhood bands its members together in conspiracy against the adult.

Thus, while she wanted terribly to grow up, she discovered satisfactions in not doing so.

Granted that we are dealing here with two *personae,* it stands to reason both that she found the material of the two masks in herself, and that she is at least tentatively trying the

masks on and speaking through them. She could at times
feel alienated from those around her, relatives and friends
and neighbors, whose existence stood in the way of her
realizing what seemed to her the full and complete being
other women had, and at the same time she could take refuge
in a disposition which forsook fulfilment but allowed her to
love and be happy with these same people. This implies an
ambivalence of sorts, but not a particularly surprising one
and not one to propose to an analyst-biographer as a
"key" to Emily Dickinson's character. Rather, it should be
suggested that these conflicting dispositions would be likely
to appear in any poet who lived and worked in similar
circumstances.

The point is that the circumstances were then remarkably
common in America, have become more so since Emily
Dickinson's time, and still persist in some degree at this
writing. Amherst was what Johnson (in his *Interpretive
Biography*, not the editions) calls a "cultural enclave."
Geographical circumstances set it apart: built on a tongue
of fertile valley floor away from the life of the main valley
and reaching toward the hills on the eastern rim, the town
had achieved a self-sufficiency, cultural and economic, which
tended to increase its effective distance from other valley
towns—like Northampton, physically only eight or nine miles
away. Such towns were on the main line of communication
to New York and the world outside, whereas Amherst was
much less so. Doubtless the isolation lessened as Amherst
changed in character during Emily Dickinson's lifetime, but
not to the extent of altering the feeling that there was, on
one hand, the little town one knew, and on the other,
opposed to it, the world outside. When one thinks of the
physical situation, one finds new poignancy in her thinking
of a poem as a "letter to the world."

Speculation about what would have happened had she

grown up in a town like Northampton (or Springfield or Hartford), instead of where she did, is inviting if otherwise unsatisfactory. In general the mores there were softer than they were in Amherst; the fact that card-playing and dancing were not entirely frowned upon there is symptomatic of a permissiveness and worldliness which had not crossed the valley. Northampton's Protestantism had not remained so rigidly formalistic, repressive, and sterile. Commerce—buying and selling—played a role in the life of Northampton such as it could not play in Amherst. People naturally moved about more. The world to which a poet might be tempted to write letters was not so far away. Would the matter of religion, to which so much of her poetry is addressed, have presented itself to her in quite such uncompromising form? Would she have been so eternally conscious of the presence and authority of her family? Would her father, seen against a background where professional men were not almost automatically the leaders of the community, have been so omnipresent in her mind? Would she have left Mount Holyoke at the end of a year? Would she have had the crucially decisive impression that there was nowhere a living audience for her poems? Perhaps the answer to all these questions, and to the many more one could ask, is negative—and perhaps, also, she would have written no poetry at all.

Such questions are empty, of course. She did not live in Northampton and that is that. But the possibility of raising them at all testifies to the importance of cultural variation in her case as in so many cases of American writers. Bridging a culture lag by moving from one kind of American community to another calls—we have seen repeatedly—for a considerable effort of readjustment, furnishes a theme, leaves a recognizable mark on writing. What we find in cases like Emily Dickinson's is that not to bridge the gulf, so long as the gulf is there, involves an adjustment also.

Some effort of adjustment would have been necessary even if she had not chosen to withdraw, undramatically and gradually but always more and more, from commerce with the community. I doubt the story that the factory whistle which disturbed the Dickinson family stirred Emily, as one critic suggests it may have done, to resent the Industrial Revolution; it is likelier that she merely disliked disturbance. But the fact remains that there was a whistle and that it disturbed. Even agricultural Amherst was not out of reach of that kind of change. It was also bound to feel the effects of increasing urbanization in the cultural bleeding-off which impoverished the areas it did not enrich. Amherst College changed its character during her lifetime, with a corresponding change in the role played by both students and faculty in the community—Amherst, a college founded in the first place so that young men could have an education without undergoing damaging contacts with the world outside. The town's population changed in nature also; for all Amherst remained Yankee, it acquired a Catholic church. And with this change came a necessary change in the status of families like the Dickinsons. No doubt Edward Dickinson remained a respected and influential figure in Amherst all his life, but respect and influence depended on the townsfolk's knowing who and what he was, depended on the fact that the values he represented stayed current, enough at least so that they accepted his evaluation of himself. And it is much to be doubted that, at the end of his life, such was the case. He was the representative of a way of life which had faded into the past. And his son, Austin, was a pallid epigone. The process by which the family reached a condition where it could become involved in an unholy row about a piece of land was a gradual one.

In other words, cultural unanimity gave way to cultural variation within the town. Emily Dickinson, to judge by the correspondence, seems to have felt the effects very little. Had she remained in closer contact with the community, she would have had to live through an experience parallel, in its quieter and less dramatic way, to the experience of the older families in Yoknapatawpha County.

7

Ezra Pound: Images of Revolt

THE LITERARY HEROES of today are the *révoltés** of day before yesterday. The French writer who studied the action of revolt and the motives of man-in-revolt most attentively and with the greatest sympathy, Camus, got the Nobel Prize just after his book on the subject—*The Rebel*—came out. And the French writer who, in his novels and studies of the psychology of art, convinced a generation that man is identifiable as man only because of his capacity for revolt, Malraux, now presides over his country's ministry of cultural affairs. No new literary movement has been launched in France, at least since the Surrealists, without the word *revolt* being used in some manifesto or other. The French make something of a poetic divinity of Rimbaud and accordingly, after Rimbaud the Catholic, Rimbaud the Surrealist, Rimbaud the Communist, and so forth, we are now invited to admire Rimbaud the first great apostle of modern revolt. And in America—perhaps more so than in England—in spite of the sad epilogue of a life so full of bewildering contradictions, a devoted and by no means small band of followers keeps green the memory of Ezra Pound.

I say *memory*, because Pound's departure from the

*The word *rebel* does not mean quite the same thing: a rebel wants to fight, whereas a true *révolté* is not sure whether he wants to fight or throw up.

111

United States must be regarded as definitive. But the memory is almost as powerful as his presence would be. I have attended a meeting of writers, critics, and professors of literature who spent an afternoon listening reverently to, and talking about, a tape-recorded message from Pound to "those who wished to understand." In the eyes of his country's justice, Pound is mad. It could be doubted if, even in the audience there assembled, there were more than one or two who took his ideas seriously. But the smell of incense was no less overpowering for all that. Tears fell as the heads swam. And it was clear that nothing guarantees a man a hearing quicker than to describe him as a *révolté*. There appears to be no straighter road to respectability.

Demonstrating this is all the easier for the fact that in America whatever distinction was once felt between mere nonconformity on one hand and revolt on the other has long since disappeared. The juveniles who lurk with switch-blades in our public parks are in revolt, but so also, apparently, are children who refuse to get to bed on time and let the telephone cool off. We talk of the revolts of the masses, of the intellectuals, of the Surrealists and Existentialists, but also of the revolt of the Southern Democrats and of the American housewife; the Beats are allegedly in revolt, but so are people like David Susskind and Robert Saudek, who merely want to do something about the incredible stupidity of television. It is too bad if the word is beyond saving, because rightly used it means something—and something important.

The notion itself of real revolt is one which fits awkwardly in the American ethos, for the very same reasons which, historically at least, make nonconformity fit so well. We are meliorists by nature. Our confidence in the possibility of improving the race has, until recently, been limitless, and is still strong: a man who refuses to pay taxes to a government which sanctions slavery, like a man who boycotts a store in the name of human rights, manifests the belief that the world will be better without slavery or that it is desirable to safeguard human rights even at the expense of considerable personal discomfort for himself. Nonconformity is, in its roundabout way, constructive, and is recognized as such. We may even encourage a certain mild eccentricity in the nonconformist. But we are entirely unprepared to deal with the individual who adopts a position of refusal, either instinctive or reasoned, toward life as we have to live it, and unprepared also to listen to the cry that somehow humanity deserves better than it gets, that the human condition is a sort of cosmic injustice. When we call a man a *révolté* we disparage him. We have never got to the point of dissociating the term from the image of the spoiled brat; it smacks of the Greenwich Village of 1913, of unwillingness to recognize routine conventions, and of relaxed sexual behavior. We are unable to recognize, as the Europeans tend to, a characterized personality type, marked by a peculiar intensity, easily exacerbated sensibilities, and an acute indisposition to compromise, capable of surveying the world around him and wanting no part of it. We can accommodate the man who says "Change it," but we cannot even hear the one who cries "To hell with it!"—and who slams the door and leaves. Our criticism has no categories for what such a personality writes because it does not occur to us that revolt may be, if not constructive, productive. And such of our potential *révoltés* as actually attempt a gesture of revolt, having no clear idea of what they are about, botch the job.

These last two statements are peculiarly relevant to the case of Ezra Pound.

What we think of Pound's poetry as a whole ultimately adds up to what we think of *Cantos*. The earlier poetry is

too manifestly clever; constantly peeking out through it is
the grinning jackanapes that Pound too often was. He was
always showing the world what he could do if he really
should set his mind to it. And to judge him in the climate his
own work created would be unfair, for Pound was always
a more accomplished poet than his work, up to and including
the Mauberley poems, revealed him to be.

He could sound as much like Browning as Browning
ever did. He could parody Housman. He could make himself
indistinguishable from W. B. Yeats playing his fiddle in
Dooney. His variations on Bertrans de Born and other
Provençal canzonists demonstrated that it was possible for
a man to be a philologist of parts without necessarily drying
up the springs of his poetry. His translations, which R. P.
Blackmur declared once to be Pound's best poetic work, also
revealed talent that perhaps should be called genius, but
even in these there is a touch of sleight of hand: for instance,
the rendering of a line of Propertius about polishing a style,
"Look, we have kept our erasers handy," can only be called
the work of a prestidigitator.

The early Pound had learned much from the medieval
jongleurs, but a *jongleur* was a juggler as well as a composer
of verses, and Pound learned too well the art of keeping a
number of sharp instruments in the air at once. The stricture
does not apply to all of his poems, of course, but to far too
many. He entrances us, but we emerge from the trance
wondering what next he will pull out of his sleeve. The
amazing, amusing Smart Aleck of the "Letters" is never far
away. The fantastically acute ear, responsible for introducing
no one knows how many new cadences to English, is too
often put to hearing puns where no one heard them before;
the poet of Audiart is the correspondent who turns the name
of James Laughlin IV's publishing enterprise into "nude
erections."

This is selling Pound short, obviously. But Pound, given the size of his talent, was selling himself short, also. We read the *Personae* today with indulgence, taking what we want ("The Seafarer" and the Mauberley poems, in my case, would be typical instances) and leaving the rest, because we know *Cantos* will be along presently. But if Pound had not at last written *Cantos,* what would he look like now other than a poet who was magnificently equipped to say something if ever he had found what it was he wanted to say? In other words, after the Mauberley poems it was time for Pound to take a subject his own size, just as Eliot had done without so much delay.

But what is the subject of *Cantos?* I mean "subject" in its simplest sense: What does the poem treat? We need to know whether there is a meaning attached to the poem as a whole beyond the sum which the meanings of individual parts may happen to add up to. The poet himself has testified on both sides: at one point he encouraged us to believe that the subjects of individual Cantos were as disparate as the subjects of conversation among intelligent men; but he also assured correspondents, very early in the composition of the work, that he had everything in hand and all would come out all right—he gave us the harassing metaphor of the ragbag which would hold anything he chose to tuck into it, but also the famous story, relayed by Yeats, of the all-inclusive diagram of the disposition of materials. Allen Tate was persuaded at the end of *XXX Cantos* that they were "about nothing." And numerous later critics, like Blackmur, have been satisfied to list the seemingly unrelated subjects of the seemingly unrelated parts. For a long time they had to be, for at first there was no way to distinguish minor themes from major ones or to recognize, from having heard them before, the varied voices in which the poet

speaks. Tate was right in what he said . . . at the moment
when he said it. But fortunately Eliot was also right, later,
in saying that with passing time *Cantos* had become
much more intelligible.

One might add, "*And* with the publication of additional
Cantos." For it is a peculiarity of the Cantos that while one
cannot see clearly enough ahead to predict where they are
going, one can see much better where they have been. They
do not have the kind of schematic structure which would
allow us to say, at the end of one section, what kind of
section would have to follow it. They have no structural
necessity of such a nature. But almost invariably, when we
finish the reading of the next section in the series we perceive
the connection with what has come previously and find, in
fact, that the earlier sections have received illumination from
the new one.

There is only one other piece of literature of which this
is so thoroughly true, *Remembrance of Things Past*. Doubtless the experience of a naïve first reading of Proust's novel
is no longer possible. We know too well, today, how the
story turns out. To remember one's puzzlement as to where
the story was going next, one's semiperception of the meanings of the thematic repetitions, one's gradual and joyful
realization—toward the end—that all the elements were falling together, dates the reader who remembers them. Only
the most veteran Proustians can recall how the significance
of the earlier sections grew upon them as they read the later
ones—and especially the great flood of illumination which
spread back over the whole work as its true subject was
finally revealed in *The Past Recaptured*.

It is too much to hope, however, that the present generation will have a similar experience with *Cantos*. There is no
verifiable sign that at the beginning Pound had any very
clear idea of how the poem would end, and too much had

happened to him in the intervening years, anyhow. His personality must have altered too much, and the look of the world must have changed for him at the same time. There is little chance of his giving us the functional equivalent of *The Past Recaptured,* and we shall never talk of *Cantos* with the sureness with which we discuss *Remembrance of Things Past.* But there is, even so, a sense in which it can be said that *Cantos* has revealed its subject as the parts have wound their slow length along.

Presumably we all agree that *Cantos* contains some sort of occult and only incompletely rational discourse. We may not look for a coherently logical argument in the work any more than we may look to Proust for a theorem about the working of time. It proceeds, rather, by the patterned juxtaposition of elements, in the way in which, as a matter of fact, so much interesting modern literature proceeds. We have to note the nature of what is juxtaposed, for it is in the contrasts between the elements that the meaning emerges, and not only from contrasts in sense but from contrasts in tone also. Thus we may get at a sort of inherent dialectic—a meaning conveyed in the structure, for the poem is constructed on these juxtapositions and whatever it is that dictates what elements shall be juxtaposed constitutes the subject of the poem.

For example, Canto LI—the second "Usura Canto"—puts next each other the eloquent enumeration of the paralyzing effects of usury and the precisely detailed directions for tying the Blue Dun and Grannom trout flies. To the reasonably alert reader two questions immediately present themselves: first, why does Pound repeat here what he said so admirably about usury in Canto XLV and, second, what are the tyings of these two trout flies doing in the poem anyhow? We are far enough along in the poem at this point to be convinced that Pound rarely stuffs such unlikely-seeming rags as these in his "ragbag" for the mere hell of it. There must be a reason for even such implausible juxtapositions as this, and I suspect very strongly that the reason lies in the very strangeness of the juxtaposition itself. The usury sequence sounds remarkably like some parts—say Jeremiah or certain Psalms—of the King James Version: indignant, full of the wrath to come, and somewhat archaic. The trout-fly descriptions are in something like the quiet language of Charles Cotton, the man who completed Walton.

The burden of the usury passage, of course, is that where bad banking practices prevail all falls apart, the center does not hold, and all endeavor which satisfies only through its own perfection is ruined. When he has said this much, Pound shifts into the placid—though again Elizabethan—tones of Cotton and, sacrificing all other effects to the communication of precise detail, displays two examples of perfectly disinterested creative effort. For neither the Blue Dun nor the Grannom is anything but a lovely piece of work to contemplate. They are both noteworthily useless, even for catching fish. One ties the Blue Dun, in particular, only because fly-tying is a traditional craft, because this fly is part of the tradition, and because one is an incomplete craftsman unless one can tie this pattern. Thus we first hear of what *usura* does, and then see samples of what it cannot do and of what it ruins. What Pound says about usury in this passage is, as has been remarked, not new in the poem; *what is new is the particular juxtaposition into which, this second time, he casts it.* For the sake of the new juxtaposition he repeats himself.

No one, so far as I can discover, has studied out all the juxtapositions in *Cantos.* Certainly I have not done so. But almost anyone who has read the Cantos with attention will agree as to the nature of the juxtapositions which have claimed his special notice: they place in contrast something from the past and something from the present, in such a way that the present is disparaged. And this fact, if I am right, will eventually lead us to the principal subject of the poem.

But first, one observation about the poem's nature. The whole thing, from one end to the other, reposes on the most hackneyed of metaphors, the familiar equation of life with a journey or voyage. After all, the poem is called *Cantos* to remind the reader of the *Divine Comedy;* whole Cantos, like the immensely obscene one about the munitions-makers, are directly reminiscent of Dante; various reminders, such as the use of "And I" (Dante's "Ed io") introducing a quotation, are planted about in other places. Dante's poem, among all the other things it is, is an allegory of life's journey. And at the same time, in the early Cantos, there is the constant reference to voyages and voyagers, the returning figure of Ulysses, the reiterations of "periplus." The nature of *Cantos* as the account of a journey is firmly established. The account, we may add, is to be accompanied by a commentary, and the burden of the commentary is that he, the voyager, has looked upon life and not found it good. This commentary is furnished by the juxtapositions of materials in the poem.

In other words, I am proposing here that the principal subject of *Cantos* as a whole poem, the only one capable of subsuming the subjects of the individual Cantos and of drawing them all into one intelligible system of meanings, is the rejection of life as it is now lived, not merely its politics and its economics but also its art, its religion, and its metaphysics. Pound began, I believe, with a rejection of our corrupt and worn-out language, and has ended by turning his back upon everything else. Those who have recently reread *Make It New* doubtless remember the surprising lines where Pound records his admiration for a writer who, he says, wrote "book after book against oppression, against all the petty sordid personal crushing oppression, the domination of modern life," and who spoke out for "human liberty, personal liberty, the rights of the individual against all sorts of intangible bondage." These lines surprise because their subject is one who usually does not strike his readers as a crusader: Henry James. Possibly Pound's judgment is wrong here; we need not care. What is important is that he is using phrases like "intangible bondage." They date from 1918, and sound as if the process of rejection had begun at that time.

Such phrases would surprise us a little if we found them in, say, the *Pisan Cantos*, because *Cantos* rejects the culture which produces the "intangible bondage." We may understand the lines

> . . . half dead at the top
> My dear William B.Y. your 1/2 was too
> moderate

to mean that against this bankruptcy of a whole culture it is not enough to be defiant and set a powerful emblem up. Yeats does not really reject; he merely laments and regrets. Something more radical is required, not merely the refusal to play, but revolt.

At one point, clearly, Pound's revolt is far from typical. In numerous ways he conforms to pattern: middle-class upbringing, somewhat special education in an esoteric subject, a first phase of artistic expression, followed by disappointment and frustration and a response to frustration in the form of a break with the kind of life previously led; he is also true to type in blaming his frustration on the conditions in which he had led his life. But revolt is a young man's game: even in the case of Gide, who is in so many ways unsatisfactory as a *révolté* but who did even so break with contemporary morality, it comes in the subject's first maturity. For Rimbaud and André Malraux, to take two textbook cases, it has aspects almost of a *rite de passage:* they enact the ritual and emerge, after a time, as individuals very different from those they were before. Pound's is a delayed reaction: born in 1885, he was approaching forty when the break came. It is not surprising that revolt should be his final phase. True to his American heritage, he was coming to his maturity rather late. It is sad that his last work should be one of a man still in the process, not of one looking back upon the process from the vantage of a final ripeness.

Cantos belongs in the category of poetry of revolt by virtue of the deeply underlying principles which determine its style and structure. This kind of work reveals the intention of achieving some sort of statement, some inexplicit expression which is not entirely contained in the materials the work brings together. Almost inevitably the result is the kind of intentional incoherence evident in Rimbaud and Malraux. Syntax, the articulation of the parts, is lacking; the parts are not adequately conjoined, co-ordinated, or subordinated in relation to each other. They are just placed side by side.

When a novelist like Malraux writes a bitter tale about men who find that they can live satisfactory lives only in the service of an ideal which is bound to destroy them, to his demonstration that the price of living a significant life is the loss of it he juxtaposes the magnificent picture of his heroes going to destruction, and the picture is noble enough to remove all the bitterness and leave behind only a feeling of enlightenment and wisdom. But while in construction *Man's Fate* is incoherent—the logic of the main parable points in one direction and the picture of the tragic outcome contradicts this logic—without the incoherence, undoubtedly, there would have been far less power in the novel.

A novelist like Céline puts his story in the mouth of a hero who cannot tell a story well, who blurts instead of talking, and whose adventures come to the readers in discontinuous fragments. Characteristically, Céline assumes that literary art—style, in this case—is a mere lie, and another instance of the universal *saloperie* of life. When he continues the biography of his hero in a second novel, periods at the ends of sentences are replaced by suspension points to show that any continuity between sentences is purely coincidental. Again, incoherence and discontinuity are fundamental to the structure of the book.

Such incoherence, of course, is never complete. We can judge incoherence only by some standard of coherence, discontinuity only by some gauge of continuity. Novels like *Journey to the End of the Night* and *Man's Fate* may *be* incoherent; they *say* something measurably coherent. In other words, their incoherence is part of their method. And if this be method, then there is not necessarily any madness in it. Those who have taken the incoherence of *Cantos* to be the first indications of mental unhealth overlook the considerable number of writers in other countries who have taken the method for their own.

Let me be the first to concede that Pound looks somewhat out of place in such distinguished company. In a sense he is indeed out of place in it; he is much more the artist than the Europeans and he is correspondingly less of an intellectual. He is obviously incapable of recognizing the difference between ideas of general significance and expressions of private and personal like and dislike; his failure to discriminate between his own predicament and the universal condition of mankind has the annoying effect of reducing his most plausible complaints against the cosmos to statements of mere individual gripe. His radical simplifications—such as the famous one which blames all the cheapness and absence of quality in modern life on the institution of usury—will not stand up against the most elementary criticism, and yet it seems obvious that criticism of even such elementary nature is far beyond the range of his capacities. In comparison even the least endowed for conceptual thinking among his French compeers, Jean Giono, whose revulsion from the ugliness and squalor of modern life is, probably, almost as instinctual and uncritical as Pound's, emerges as his intellectual superior. Most of the literature of revolt, including even the work of Céline, maintains a kind of dignity, whereas Pound's persistence in putting so much lore and erudition at the service of so few brains keeps his own dignity, and that of his work, in constant peril.

But *Cantos* becomes much more intelligible, I think, as soon as we recognize that it belongs in this category. Otherwise one is always plagued by the seeming irrelevance of certain parts of the poem to the rest. We have to deal with the "Chinese" Cantos as well as the "Pisan," and those insufferable ones which Hugh Kenner labels Adamic and Jeffersonian; we have to cope with the problems created by the opening of a bank at Siena and those created by the tales of the exploits of Renaissance plug-uglies like Sigismondo Malatesta; we have to reconcile ourselves to the appeals for an oriental kind of order in the midst of a disorderly poem and discover *some* significance in Jim X's telling the Banker-Deacons of Chicago the Tale of the Honest Sailor. And *Cantos* as poem does not furnish us the help we need.

I find myself unable to work up much agreement with the claim of some Poundians that the reader does not need the help of glosses to get him through *Cantos;* and for the work of the group at Northwestern University who have been compiling and circulating in mimeograph the requisite supplementary information, I would like my gratefulness on record. Pound has spent a lifetime reading; he knows a lot; and he is no man to leave what he knows out of his poetry. Who but Pound could expect the reader to know, for instance, what he intends in the reference to Shoeney's

daughters in Canto II? Unless one has read somewhere
about the source, and knows also that the eccentric spelling
is Pound's own, the job is hopeless. We may not feel that
all Pound's erudition is useful to the poem, and at times we
may feel that he is merely parading it; even so, we have to
put up with it, and for any relief much thanks. More than
we have had to date would be welcome. But I don't see how
any amount of it can open the poem completely to us unless
we realize also the meaningful discontinuity—or incoherence
—of revolt.

So I am arguing that we have to read *Cantos* somewhat
as we read that other masterpiece of discontinuity, Céline's
Journey to the End of the Night. Céline sends his hero down
the dark corridor of life, looking anxiously for some glimmer
of light. In rare instances he catches a momentary flicker—
the sergeant growing a few rachitic flowers in the African
wilds and sending home his pay to care for a relative's
child; Molly, the honest whore in Detroit, with her instinctive
kindliness. But the rest of life is only the *saloperie*, the tan-
gible as well as the intangible bondage. Pound's poet moves
along his "periplus," until it becomes finally a "periplus" in
a camion full of prisoners. His present is Céline's darkness;
the flashes of light are from the past. The integrity of John
Adams, the humaneness of Hapsburg-Lorraine, Kung's vision
of order, My Cid riding up to Burgos, leave the darkness
only deeper after they have flared for a moment and died
again. *Donna mi prega* illumines just by being beautiful . . .
and inaccessible now that the maid's needle has been blunted.
And if the poem is consistently ironic because the method
of juxtapositions is inherently an ironic one, and also because
after speaking again and again in an assumed voice the
poet reveals that the assumed voice is really a deformation
of his own, it is also pathetic because the things which
might relieve the darkness are so thoroughly lovely and

desirable but at the same time so thoroughly out of reach.

Taken as an expression of revolt, *Cantos* seems to me to be a very great poem, second among its kind only to Rimbaud's *Season*. Because of its nature it will rarely be known in its entirety and because of its subject many readers will never be able to take it for anything but a historical document. They will think it a monstrosity, and they will be right; to a certain extent, monstrosity is implied by the subject itself. Other readers will object, so long as the poem has readers at all, to the parts which give evidence of Pound's almost unlimited self-indulgence, his willingness to run on eternally on his favorite subjects, his affectations (including the part of his erudition which is affected), his use of the Chinese characters which he has to clip from a dictionary and stick to his manuscript because he is unable to draw them well himself, and other similar annoyances. They will be right, in a degree, also. But so will those who insist that in *Cantos* Pound has done something that is worth doing and that has never been done before.

Yet our attitudes toward him would have been infinitely less ambivalent if his revolt had come somewhat closer to following the recognized pattern.

Revolt, as generally understood by those who stop to think about it—and as formally defined by Camus—consists of saying No, i.e. of refusing to live life as we have known it, of refusing what the French like to call our human condition. The textbook case is undoubtedly Ivan Karamazov, rejecting a world whose perfection would entail the suffering of a single helpless being.

"I challenge you—answer. Imagine that you are creating a fabric of human destiny with the object of making men happy in the end, giving them peace and rest at last. Imagine that you are doing this but that it is essential and inevitable to torture to death only one tiny creature—that child beating its breast with its fist, for instance—in order to found that edifice on its unavenged tears. Would you consent to be the architect on those conditions?"

Even to the gentle brother Alyosha the reply has to be an automatic and complete negative. The consequence of revolt is of course defeat. But if he must go down, the *révolté* goes down in unmitigated defiance of Ivan's sort: his prototypes are Prometheus and Milton's Satan. Pound sees his own prototype to be not Prometheus, and much less Satan, but Ulysses. Even those who find little good to say of him must be somewhat touched by the half-hidden references to himself as the man grown old, and beaten by much voyaging, in the later Cantos.

Periplus, indeed: Hailey, Idaho, Hamilton College, the University of Pennsylvania, Italy, France, and Spain, the stay in London, then Paris, and after that Rapallo . . . before Pisa, Washington, D.C., and the final exile. But never, his biographers say, did he accept life away from home as a final answer. Always his eyes were on America; always, wherever he was, he was an American visitor, an outsider from Elsewhere. The door did not slam but drew gradually closed. And we cannot be sure that in his private life as an entity his revolt was as clear-cut and decisive as it was in the poetry; even there, in fact, it does not seem entirely consistent. Charles Norman's recent book leaves open the possibility that the content of the Fascist broadcasts did not greatly differ from what was being said in the United States by some of the political enemies of Franklin D. Roosevelt. What is certain is that instead of reaching the point of revolt at the age, a youthful one, when typical *révoltés* reach it he came to it slowly, in middle life. The picture one cannot help drawing is of the recognizable, melioristic American nonconformist hardening gradually into something else, coming bit by bit to the point of saying No.

Doubtless we do not yet know the whole story, but all this begins to sound like another one of the epics of displacement. Pound's life *could* be interpreted as affected by the inevitable need to adjust to new circumstances. He would have to be placed among the special category of those who have had, also, to adjust to being American when they were outside the country's borders. Clearly his work is not a treatment of what I have called our Great Topos, but just possibly it could be read as an interesting footnote on the subject.

There is a wealth of suggestion in comparing him with a European who has made a literary fortune from revolt, like Malraux. Born (1901) in Paris, socially middle class, educated at the Lycée Condorcet, Malraux began writing as a Surrealist a year or so in advance of his time. Then, suddenly, he was off for Indochina with a young wife and some plans for finding deserted temples. He found them, fought bitterly with colonial officials over the proceeds, nearly went to jail, spent eight months editing a French language newspaper at Saigon during which he joined forces with the left wing of the Kuomintang. He may have had some connection with the insurrection of 1926 in Canton, but stories grow vague on the subject of his exact role. As suddenly as he had left he turned up again in France, but now as the author of writings which his early Surrealism hardly led one to expect: novels, characterized by violence of action and by their atmosphere of tragedy. Then came Malraux's ten years of warfare, first in Spain against Franco, then in France against Hitler. A break with the Communists was followed by an abandonment of imaginative literature: the one novel he began after 1936 had never been finished. Instead, once out of uniform he went back to the study of art and the writing of *The Psychology of Art, The Voices of Silence, The Metamorphosis of the Gods.* At the end of the war he had met de Gaulle and been, momentarily, a minister in the latter's coalition cabinet. After the events of 1958 in Algiers and the installation of de Gaulle's Fifth Republic he became a minister again and, at this writing, is one still.

Compared with the crisp decisiveness of every turn in Malraux's career, the wanderings of Pound's give one the feeling of following a cow-path. The year 1958 will go down as the one when Pound went back to Rapallo. There has been no triumph of justice or of injustice. A court had found, twelve years earlier, that he was mentally incapable of defending himself; it now declared that, in the eyes of the law, he would never be able to do so. All the painful ambiguities and uncertainties of the case remain, however. Nothing has really been settled.

Yet it is easier to write about him now than it was while he was still shut up in St. Elizabeths Hospital. His case had been tried too abundantly in the newspapers. The organs of American Philistinism, led by *Time,* had convinced too many that modern poetry was on trial with him. Especially after the award of the Bollingen Prize, with the attendant outcry from the *Saturday Review* and similar periodicals, anything said about Pound's poetry was bound to be taken either as a plea for setting him loose without further legal formality, or else as a demand that he should be taken forthwith before a firing squad.

Under the strain the situation generated, few managed to write about Pound with anything like appropriate dispassion. Hugh Kenner's *The Poetry of Ezra Pound* is full of useful information and keen insights, but normally mild reviewers have gone on record as finding it full, also, of bumptious nonsense. Kenner stopped some digestions completely with his declaration that some three hundred years ago English poetry went off on the wrong track and has

had to wait out the long interval for Pound to put it right.
But his pro-Pound extravagance was matched, as other
normally mild reviewers again noted, by the anti-Pound
extravagance of Rossell Hope Robbins' *The T. S. Eliot Myth*
and the argument that it is impossible to write good poetry
if one holds bad political ideas—a thesis which would disqualify much poetry from Hesiod to the present. Anyone
else writing about Pound, except for largely factual accounts
like the excellent one by Hayden Carruth in *Perspectives
USA*, felt the danger of being forced into one camp or the
other, of being taken to line up beside Kenner or beside
Robbins. It was hard to find a place to stand alone.

It is good that this condition has changed. Pound had
been that rarest phenomenon, a bellwether for a generation
of poets who was also a considerable poet in his own right.
He was a more genuine leader of movements, for example,
than Amy Lowell, and his poetry was better, too. None of
it may be so compelling as the best of Eliot's, but for a
moment he had been Eliot's master—the *miglior fabbro* of
The Waste Land—and he had had the public personality
to play the role of the embattled poet among the Philistines
as the less flamboyant Eliot never could. Some of his criticism
is still good reading, years after the event; and his correspondence, even in the incomplete and defective edition
available, is perhaps the liveliest and most revealing since
Flaubert's. And in his moments of generosity he was an
accomplished chivvier of publishers, a stout rescuer of distressed literary reviews, and a support for men like William
Butler Yeats.

If he had not set up, many years ago, as an expert on
the subject for which, of all possible subjects, he was the
least equipped, economics; if he had not adopted the
thoroughly unacceptable politics which was the only one
in which his distributist economics could reasonably be

expected to work; if he had not allowed his politics to sanction his broadcasting over the Italian radio—if, in other words, he had behaved reasonably in spheres remote from poetry—some of his poetry would be different, of course, but he would be venerated, if not understood, at this writing. From such dilemmas as, in historical fact, Pound forced upon us, there is no pleasant exit. A simpler time than ours might have shot the broadcaster and enshrined the poet without experiencing any uncomfortably contradictory emotions. Ours cannot. At the end of World War II, the French shot Robert Brasillach and imprisoned Charles Maurras for life; neither solution now seems to have been satisfactory. Pound did not even get his day in court.

Neither did we, his readers, although we needed, in a way, the cleansing experience of a verdict more than Pound did. We did not get it—and are permanently denied release from our own ambivalences. The best we can do at this point is to discipline ourselves into becoming a dispassionate, detached audience capable of an effort toward understanding. The fact that the figure of the *révolté* looms so large in modern literature, and that revolt has forced itself on us as one of the dominant themes in modern writing, presents us with an obligation. Not to face it would be to surrender a chance to understand ourselves.

Facing it would appropriately begin with the admission that Pound is a completely American phenomenon. And if it has turned out that his revolt has been lopsided and incompletely decisive, this is undoubtedly an American phenomenon also. What makes revolt possible and plausible —and even easy—is a cultural uniformity so great that the potential *révolté* can reject his whole culture at once. Metaphysical revolt would make sense only as a subsequent step. To judge by such examples as Rimbaud and Malraux, the step is even inconceivable otherwise. In a culture which is the opposite of uniform, the cry of the *révolté* will be hard to distinguish from the cry of the Displaced. And we shall undoubtedly go on using the word *revolt* to describe the discontent of housewives and the uneasiness of the very young.

8

Jack Kerouac and the Beats

THERE IS probably a lot about the Beat Generation which is not the doing of Jack Kerouac, just as there is probably a lot about Kerouac which has nothing to do with, and should not be held against, the Beats as a group; but Kerouac is undeniably more responsible than anyone else for the public image of the Beats current at this writing. *On the Road, The Dharma Bums,* and *The Subterraneans* are easy to get and to read, because they are novels and in paperback, whereas the work of most of the others who wear the Beatnik label is poetry, not available on the newsstands, and thus not so widely read. And books like Lawrence Lipton's *The Holy Barbarians* are likely to be read by people who, for the most part, are already committed to an interest in the subject. So, whether or not it is fair to the Beats or to Jack Kerouac, our general notion of the New Abstention cannot but come from his novels—in particular, because it has been the most widely read, from *On the Road.*

The result is a certain distortion. Kerouac deals in the picturesque, specializing in the area of the Beatnik way of life which is the most likely to hold the attention of the Square, the part which it is easiest to dig. Like the spreads in the big news weeklies and picture magazines, which invariably show the most evidently hip of cats sprawling in —or is it on?—the most dilapidated pads, what he offers to our gaze is the membership of the vanguard, which is indistinguishable from the lunatic fringe. As the protesting Letters to the Editor which follow each such *Time-Newsweek-Look-Life* story argue very loudly, the public is being invited to take a part for the whole. By the kind of cultural synecdoche which invariably operates in such instances, the people in Kerouac's books are coming to stand for a nobody knows how much larger segment of the total population, a less conspicuous body of literate Americans—particularly artists, writers, musicians, architects, and other such—whose ways of living do not necessarily force them to wear the gray flannel livery, who have grown increasingly disaffected from ordinary American life, and who persist in thinking and living just about as they like and with no particular deference to our existing folkways, mores, and norms. The value of Kerouac's novels is that they incarnate in a visible shape a phenomenon which would otherwise be very hard to see, just as the danger of them is that in distorting the picture for their purpose—an entirely legitimate purpose, since Kerouac's business is literature and not journalistic sociology—they make the new development look more frivolous and less significant than it may well turn out to be.

Few of us Squares have any idea where the "beat" in Beat Generation comes from, whether it is beat as in music or as in all beat up or as in dead-beat, but our ignorance is not particularly important since the Beats obviously don't know, either. And in turn, it may be just as well that they don't, since if one meaning applied better than the others the Beat Generation would not be the vague, slithering, amorphous thing it so clearly is. To begin with, it is not *one* generation but *two:* the older Beats were in uniform during World War II, whereas some of the younger ones were not of draft age for Korea. Kerouac, himself, is approaching forty, and by the time one is forty a new generation is breathing down one's neck. Kenneth Rexroth is still older. We had better stop worrying the word "generation" and concentrate on the word "Beat."

Here again there is trouble, for there is no dependable way to distinguish the Bohemians of North Beach and Venice West from those who a decade back frequented the sidewalks near Saint-Germain-des-Prés. In both cases you will find the same ostentatiously inexpensive clothes worn as a uniform, the beards, the lank hair, the same noctambulance, the same air of fatigue, the same love of jazz, the same semiprivate language. There is, admittedly, a perceptible difference between Sartre's Existentialism and Zen—the same difference as between *engagement* and disengagement—but not much chance that the adherents of one or the other can tell you what it is; except in rare instances they don't care. And between the individuals themselves there is even less chance of drawing a line: many of the older Beats worked an apprenticeship in Paris.

So the best one can finally produce is the impression that the Beats aren't really a historical generation, and can't be told apart from their immediate predecessors, and don't know any better than we do what their name means, so that all in all we turn out to be trying to understand a label for the current, local manifestation of an international tendency which will shortly have survived two decades without giving verifiable signs of exhaustion.

So the most palpable fact about the Beat Generation, and probably the most important one, is merely that it exists, has existed for a considerable time, and promises to continue existing until the conditions which have brought it into being shall themselves markedly change. The Beats have been kidded, criticized, and drummed out of the regiment; alternately they are condemned as juvenile delinquents

who have refused to grow up—thus a considerable danger—
or dismissed as without consequence and beneath notice.
Such misjudgments are probably without importance, even
though it is true that Allen Ginsberg and Gregory Corso,
Kenneth Patchen and Kenneth Rexroth have written more
excellent poetry than the Square press suspects, and although
this is just as true as that Kerouac has written more deplor-
able prose than even Kerouac himself suspects. But it happens to be true also that if any breeze now stirs our cultural
doldrums it is the Beats who are stirring the air.

To say the same thing in another way, what is most
alive in our culture is what wants absolutely nothing to
do with it. In the vocabulary of the present discussion, the
Beats, like everybody else, have come up against the
problem of adjustment to America, but unlike everybody
else they have decided that the effort of adjustment isn't
worth the trouble. In the midst of a civilization which
awards all its prizes to conformity, and which, if what
we read about it is true, could do nothing else, here they
just sit—when not gadding on the Road—unwilling (or
unable, what difference?) to conform, wanting only to be
let alone in their nonbelligerent nonparticipation. Some
of the alienated voices are raucous, and many are off-key,
but they are characteristically difficult to tune out.

Properly speaking, these are not the voices of revolt.
Here, for example, is a highly representative character in
what I take to be Kerouac's best book, *The Dharma Bums:*

"I've been reading Whitman, know what he says, *Cheer
up slaves, and horrify foreign despots,* he means that's the attitude
for the Bard, the Zen Lunacy bard of old desert paths, see the
whole thing is a world full of rucksack wanderers, Dharma Bums
refusing to subscribe to the general demand that they consume
production and therefore have to work for the privilege of con-
suming, all that crap they didn't really want anyway such as

refrigerators, TV sets, cars, at least new fancy cars, certain hair oils and deodorants and general junk you finally always see a week later in the garbage anyway, all of them imprisoned in a system of work, produce, consume, work, produce, consume, I see a vision of a great rucksack revolution thousands or even millions of young Americans wandering around with rucksacks, going up to mountains to pray, making children laugh and old men glad, making young girls happy and old girls happier, all of 'em Zen Lunatics who go about writing poems that happen to appear in their heads for no reason and also by being kind and also by strange unexpected acts keep giving visions of eternal freedom to everybody and to all living creatures . . ."

The speaker happens to be a little drunk, but his views are not greatly different when he is sober. He sounds in some ways very like the Steinbeck of going-on thirty years ago, who wrote *The Grapes of Wrath*. (In some moods Kerouac, too, is in fact very like Steinbeck: he loves people, especially simple people, and he is against whatever pushes them around.) There is no suggestion of the *révolté's* definitively slammed door, of shaking the dust off his feet, of going elsewhere for good and all. The Beat just wants no part of what he calls "the rat race." Except for an occasional bleat from someone like Ginsberg, he can hardly be said to protest. Rather, he abstains. His alienation is passive.

One of the reasons why the Beats are hard to understand is that we have had so little experience in America with Bohemias in general. Our only previous one of any significance was in Greenwich Village just before and for a few years after World War I, a strictly metropolitan phenomenon. Most of America knew about it only what got into the newspapers or occasional novels. After that, our nearest approach was the retreat of the Expatriates to Paris and the Mediterranean islands; and this again was something special, largely because the Sad Young Men and their female counterparts were such nice, clean-necked young people, and dressed without discrediting Brooks Brothers; theirs was a Harvard and Princeton migration, and, besides, most of them went abroad to work worthily and hard. We are perhaps still too innocent to realize that Bohemias have been essential ever since the Industrial Revolution changed the fundamental economics of the arts.

For a long time it has been true that unless the artist has been kept either by his family or by an institution, he has not had the time, even when he has kept the inclination, to enter the general competition; he has had to live where living is cheap and where a minimum expenditure of energy will keep him sheltered and fed. The solution, at one time or another, has been Belgravia, Montmartre, the Left Bank, the Village. Responsible critics like Malcolm Cowley have tried for years to get the public to understand this fact in the case of the Expatriates, but it was equally true of the Romantic Bohemians of Murger; and it is just as true of the people along North Beach.

Such life has the additional merit, no less genuine for being less easily measurable, of providing a status of its own which lets one out of the eternal struggle for status. Bohemian dress is not only inexpensive, but is also not a gray flannel suit and is thus a badge. Wearing it, one announces to the world that one is not bound by the rules of the Game. The wearer belongs to a separate caste. At times the great middle class, by which name he identifies those he is unlike, has been his enemy; it has never been his friend.

To Bohemia are also attracted numerous characters who do not paint or compose or sculpture or write, but who like the life and the atmosphere because they are comfortable and happy in it. For every Beat who is artistically productive there are many who do not even perform on the Bongo drum, just as once there were Expatriates who merely took up space at the Dôme and the Coupôle. Some of them join up because they enjoy the relaxation of morals and the transfer of social disapproval, when there is any, from the individual to the group. And like the artists, they are glad not to compete for status. Lawrence Lipton's estimate, that there are a hundred nonperforming Beats for every writer, artist, or musician, may be high, but one may doubt its being far off the mark. And he is talking only about completely identifiable Beats. The proportion may not have been much lower in the various other Bohemias the world has known.

What is new in Bohemia is that, since World War II, life and love have become infinitely less dangerous than they used to be. A century ago the risk was much higher. Living in unheated and unclean quarters, and in an unfavorable climate, eating bad food irregularly, absorbing more than his share of popular-priced intoxicants, and not getting enough sleep, the olden time Bohemian could count on tuberculosis, syphilis, and a number of other occupational hazards. Today the society from which he separates himself goes right on, in its mindless charity, with unemployment insurance, free clinics, and all the other public beneficences to which the Beat may turn if trouble comes. The Beats are, as a matter of fact, the first recalcitrant group ever supported by government subsidy—meaning the G.I. Bill, the 25-20 Club, and unemployment benefits.

It would not be surprising if there turned out to be a connection between the current affluence of the economy and the most striking characteristic of the Beats—their not being angry. Early Bohemias have been hotbeds of radical doctrine. The artist's feeling of separation from his class led easily to hostility, most often theoretical but sometimes active. Anarchism and the various forms of socialism flourished. One might not be personally disposed to plunge into a struggle to save the world, but one was surely not disposed to be unsympathetic to those who did. Today, among the Beats, no such tendency gains headway. Like Rinehart in the song, they are most indifferent guys, probably because they are under no pressure to be anything else.

Aside from this absence of socio-political protest, times have changed in the last thirty years surprisingly less than one would think. Our coevals who urged us, after the Crash, to unite with the workers of the world objected to most of the things the Beats object to: waste in the economy, the meaninglessness of much of the work offered by an industrial society, uneven distribution of the total take, Philistinism, the crassness of going status symbols. Distribution is somewhat better than it used to be, but the rest does not seem to be greatly different. Yet whereas an earlier generation stomped off scowling to the public library to read the *New Masses,* the Beat retires voluntarily to the present equivalent of a Hooverville, strums a guitar, smokes a bit of "tea," works up his Zen. This unwillingness or inability to react probably explains why Kerouac's novels so frequently irritate his older readers.

The story of *The Subterraneans* has been written several thousand times. Boy loves girl and love would seem to promise happiness, but love cannot support the weight of success. The girl has a couple of disabilities: she is a Negro and in constant need of psychiatric care. The boy has a gift which makes him a considerable literary figure, but is such a complete paranoid that, while physically harmless, he is impossible to deal with. After a while he gets so awful that even his crazy mistress can't stand him any longer; she goes to another man, and our hero has nothing left to do but write a book on how happy he was once and how happy he now isn't.

Leave out the local and topical nature of the disabilities and what is left is a plot worn out by European writers

before 1860. The consumption of which heroines once died
has mutated into psychosis; the inertia of the hero and his
inability to take himself by the scruff of the neck and make
himself behave is explained in new words, with more syl-
lables in each; in other aspects everything is remarkably
familiar. The Beats are a recognizable Romantic generation.

But in Romantic literature the hero and heroine are
right and the world is wrong, whereas with the Beats nobody
is right and the world is just what it happens to be, something
that nothing can be done about, but that you have to live
with. Misfortunes come from the way the ball bounces, the
way the cloth tears. Leo the hero is such an unpleasant
type that Kerouac could, if he cared to, sue the reviewers
misguided enough to assume that, because Leo is a writer of
French-Canadian origin who has been merchant seaman
and railroad man, there is something autobiographical
about him and his story. But the important point is not
that he is so outrageous, but that he blames nobody else
for his being so, and that at the same time, so far as his own
responsibility is concerned, he just feels that he can't help
it: some people are born to be lice and that is the last word
on the subject. The Romantic image of the self as victim
is missing.

In Kerouac's novels, it must be admitted, the Beat
hero's image of himself is never entirely clear. Even his
separateness from the rest of society—what society calls
his "maladjustment"—does not strike Kerouac as particularly
momentous. What seems mostly to be on the novelist's mind
is the special quality of the life the Beats live. The chances
are ten to one that the sales of Kerouac's novels result
largely from the curiosity of the non-Beat, Square public
about this same style of living; we all want to know about
flips and pads and cats, and it is in fact high time that
we did begin to dig them. In the circumstances it would be

unfair to accuse Kerouac, and the Beats in general, of exhibitionism.

No doubt a certain amount of exhibitionism characterizes the Beats. It characterizes most Bohemian attitudes. But it should be added that in such instances there is always some public curiosity to exploit and that nothing in the Beat credo forbids profiting by it. The so-called "Lost Generation," likewise, knew that it had the public's attention, and offered no more objection than the Beats do. *The Sun Also Rises* sold copiously, at least in the beginning, to people primarily interested in finding out what life was like in Paris. And who will affirm that Hemingway's story of the love of a eunuch for a nymphomaniac did not appeal to some as pruriently esoteric?

But there are, after all, two differences which should be underlined. The Lost Generation numbered some very stern moralists, Hemingway among them. Hemingway hated the phony and was obsessed by what he called "integrity." The people in *The Sun Also Rises* did not have integrity. With the exception of one, the bullfighter Pedro Romero, they were "rotten." There are as many evocations of rot, as many images of decay, in this novel as there are in *Hamlet*. Similarly, Lieutenant Henry, on the verge of making his "separate peace" and running away with Catherine, will declare that war is rotten; and in *To Have and Have Not* the rottenness of the American rich will be the background of the sincere, desperate violence of Harry Morgan. Nick Carraway, assuring Gatsby of the latter's superiority to Tom, Daisy, and the rabble who come to the big parties, uses the same word: "They are all rotten." Possibly the moral standard is not a complex one, but the reader will look far to find anything even suggestive of it in the work of the Beats. If Kerouac's picture is accurate, they seem entirely uninterested in ethical considerations.

The same has to be said about aesthetic standards, also. That the Lost Generation was rigorous in the demands it made on its own writing has long since become a cliché. Its members were busy, as MacLeish puts it, whittling out their styles. The Beats, on the other hand, seem easily satisfied with what they turn out. Why develop a style of your own when almost anyone else's style can be appropriated?

...I come out to tell Mardou we have decided to take later train in order to go back to house to pick up forgotten package which is just another ringaroundtherosy of futility for her, she receives this news with solemn lips—ah my love and lost darling (out of date word)—if then I'd known what I know now, instead of returning to bar, for further talks, and looking at her with hurt eyes, etc., and let her lay there in the bleak sea of time untended and unsolaced and unforgiven for the sin of the sea of time I'd have gone in and sat down with her, taken her hand, promised her my life and protection—"Because I love you and there's no reason"—but then far from having completely successfully realized this love, I was still in the act of thinking I was climbing out of my doubt about her—but the train came, finally, 153 at 5:31 after all our delays, we got in, and rode to the city—through South San Francisco and past my house, facing one another in coach seats, riding by the big yards in Bayshore and I gleefully (trying to be gleeful) point out a kicked boxcar ramming a hopper and you see the tinscrap shuddering far off, wow—but most of the time sitting bleakly under either stare and saying, finally, "I really do feel I must be getting a rummy nose"—anything I could think of saying to ease the pressure of what I really wanted to weep about—but in the main the three of us really sad, riding together on a train to gayety, horror, the eventual H bomb.

This is a page from *The Subterraneans,* near the end of the story where Leo's affair with Mardou is collapsing; their situation has deteriorated considerably during the party at Los Altos from which they are returning. I would apologize for the length of the quotation, except that the fault is

inherent in the passage itself: inspection will show that
there is no place to cut off the flow without being suspect
of making the writing look worse than it is. The syntax, we
may take it, is modeled on Faulkner's. At least, one may
doubt that Kerouac would have risked a nonstop sentence
of this sort if Faulkner's example had not encouraged him
to think he could get away with it, and one recognizes
Faulkner's insistent use of the gerund to enforce the feeling
of continuity, of things happening one right after another
and felt by the consciousness not as discrete events but
as a flow, one running into the next. But Faulkner uses
his syntax as an instrument for organizing brute experience,
for revealing the relationships between seemingly unrelated
parts of it and thus for reducing its incoherence, whereas
Kerouac's does little more than link the pieces of experience
end to end, is loose where Faulkner's—for all his unorthodoxy
—is tight, and in places keeps going only by benefit of comma
fault. Meanwhile, the business about the bleak sea of time
"untended and unsolaced and unforgiven" and the sin of
the sea of time (whatever *that* is) suggests the example of
Wolfe. The series of small but momentarily important sense-
impressions, as the train approaches the city, sound as if
Kerouac had been reading Hemingway. And the finale,
about the destination of the train, "gayety, horror, the
eventual H bomb," has all the irrelevance of Fitzgerald
ending *The Great Gatsby*.

But just as the Faulknerian syntax is really pseudo-
Faulknerian, the Wolfe-ish bit uses words Wolfe might
use without anything of his elevation or seriousness or
eloquence, the sensory detail is not urgently sharp as it
is in Hemingway's writing when he is good, and the bit
that reminds one of Fitzgerald is reminiscent of Fitzgerald
at his weakest. Apparently Kerouac has the taste to choose
his masters well but feels no impulsion to learn much from

them. In total effect, his prose is hyper-literary and at the same time somewhat ignorant.

The spirit of Faulkner hovers over his whole book, in that from the first page there is the effort to establish the narrating "voice" as the organizing force—telling the story, arranging the fragments of experience, imposing emotions on the reader, setting the characteristic tone. But the continual variations between the hyper-literary, the not-literary-at-all, and even the anti-literary make the tone inconsistent. One finishes the novel with a feeling of having waded through a good deal of untidy craftsmanship and just plain messiness, and is convinced that Faulkner, Wolfe, Hemingway, and Fitzgerald, for all the fault we have found with them, were of another order of magnitude. It is a pity, not so much that Kerouac does not write better, but that he seems not to care about writing better. It is in this sense that the Beats are as unmoved by aesthetic imperatives as they are by moral ones.

The blurb on the cover of *The Subterraneans* asserts that Kerouac "burst" upon the American literary world. This is not true: he sidled in, quietly, as the necessary and inevitable spokesman of a group or a movement (though neither group nor movement in the ordinary sense) which was by its nature bound to produce a spokesman eventually. Writing carelessly, he arrived less with a bang than with a whimper. A thunderously good novel would have made bang enough to persuade a larger public that a prevalence of Beats in this country means something.

Whether we like it or not, they personify nonconformity at a time when nonconformity has unusual value, and their nonconformity is authentically, unmistakably American, and attached to the central tradition. One of their gods is Whitman, and through him they go back to Emerson and Concord, where nonconformity still has its shrine. Another is

Rimbaud, and again, since Rimbaud looks back to Baudelaire and Baudelaire in turn looks back and across the ocean
to Emerson (among others, of course), we end up again in
Concord. Few literary movements could claim more distinguished ancestry, or a more authentic family tree. But
precisely because the identification with America is so
complete, the extent to which the tradition of nonconformity
has degenerated stands out especially clear.

Twenty or thirty years ago our nonconformists were men
like John Dos Passos and Granville Hicks, one a novelist of
great, though uneven, power and the other a well-informed
and extremely literate critic. Neither of them was or is to be
confused with Emerson, but both were men of rigorous
aesthetic standards, and the political attitudes of both were
based on an indignation which was clearly moral in nature.
They treated their own alienation with respect, shoring it up
with serious ideas seriously handled, writing what they did
from the vantage point of knowledge acquired by effort,
working at their nonconformity. In comparison the Beats
are unimpressive.

There is something symbolic about Beatnik allegiances
in music. They are, everyone knows, addicted to jazz—so far
as I can see, both an honorable and a valuable addiction,
since jazz seems to exercise a deep and beneficial influence
upon their poetry. But the Beats are not jazz men themselves.
To be a good jazz man is a professional accomplishment,
requiring much work toward the gradual perfecting of
technique; the jazz man may be self-tutored but he is not
untutored, and he works with an instrument which has to
be mastered. But when the Beat starts making music, his
characteristic instrument is the guitar. I know that there
are distinguished guitarists in the world; it remains a fact
that if you cannot pick strings artfully you can still strum,
and strumming can be learned in a very short time indeed—

one just buys a "chord book." There is nothing wrong with autodidacticism in itself, but a lot could be said against putting it in the service of easy superficiality. The auto-didacticism of Henry Miller has given us some important books. But it is a far cry from the work of Miller to that of some of his epigoni, and the distance is to be equated with devoted work.

One curious pattern which is repeated in Kerouac's novels may turn out to mean a great deal. There is, in each one, the first person narrator who controls the point of view and is at the center of the important events; and then there is a second character toward whom the narrator takes a peculiarly respectful attitude, like Dean Moriarty in *On the Road* and Japhy in *The Dharma Bums*. These latter the narrator treats as initiates in the mystery in which he is something, himself, of a neophyte—as potential guides and mentors in life. It would be tempting to talk about the kind of admiration a younger schoolboy sometimes conceives for an older one or even of some attachment to a father-substitute, but the fact is that Dean Moriarty is the narrator's age and that Japhy is about ten years younger! This would seem to preclude any quick and easy explanation of the relationship, but not to diminish its importance. Kerouac's character, age or no age, is taking the stance of a younger man looking up to one who, despite his actual years, exudes the kind of mastery over life which comes from knowing what is what. Whether the character in question actually possesses any such mastery is, of course, entirely beside the point: what is relevant is the narrating character's willing-ness, not to say his determination, to place himself in the junior position. To label any such disposition an intentional rejection of maturity might be to presume too much, and give to a simple observation the dignity of a diagnosis. Not to notice it at all would be lamentable blindness. It is disturbing that, approaching forty, Kerouac should instal in his third novel this same pattern which is central in his first one. An unsympathetic critic, aware that the position of the Beats is formulated in terms of their throwing up the whole question of adjustment to life in America as not worth the candle, and finding, first, that Kerouac's heroes are disposed to resist growing up completely, and, second, that Kerouac himself rejects the ordinary obligations of a writer toward his craft, might be disposed to insist upon the possible cause and effect relationships involved.

On the whole, the Beats deserve a more accomplished spokesman than Kerouac has been to date. And at the same time, everyone else's view of what was going on in America would be clearer if he did not leave it possible for his books to be read as mere curiosities or as documents on life along the neurotic fringe. For in addition to the picturesque Beat of North Beach or Venice West there exists also the unpicturesque Beat of everywhere else, who may even be the Beat in the Gray Flannel Suit, not very happy about life but not particularly psychopathic either, and identifiable only if one knows him well enough to know how completely he is disaffected. He is the Disorganization Man, whom the social scientists do not have the opportunity to count, whose character is not subsumed in Riesman's oxymoron of the lonely crowd. One could wish that, knowing the feelings of the Beat as well as he does, Kerouac could also find himself capable of writing a novel which would get down far deeper beneath the surface than he has so far probed, working more carefully with whatever it is that all Beats—whether they flaunt the Beat uniform or not—have in common. The resulting novel might frighten where the previous ones just amuse, but the chances are that in addition it would document, perhaps very surprisingly, Riesman's observation that no culture is "all of a piece."

9

The Dilemmas of Criticism

THE *Harvard Gazette* of November 5, 1960, announcing the inaugural lecture of Harry Levin as the first Irving Babbitt Professor of Comparative Literature, included the following paragraph to explain the naming of the chair:

> Professor Babbitt . . . taught French literature at Harvard from 1894 until his death in 1933. During this period he introduced the comparative study of the literature of different traditions and became a major intellectual force in America and an exponent of the New Humanism of the 1920's. His book *Literature and the American College* (1908) still influences the teaching of the humanities, and his *Rousseau and Romanticism* (1919) is considered a major literary study. His social and political philosophy were outlined in *Democracy and Leadership* (1924).

In spite of the obvious implication, Babbitt is not completely forgotten in Cambridge. The last generation to sit in his classes and chorus back, as he required, his tendentious definitions of critical terms, is at the peak of its intellectual activity. Yet he is not often mentioned, possibly because those who might refer to him have reached an age where apoplexy is no remote menace; and he had that about him which turned some mild and normally reasonable men apoplectic. And the very fact that some members of the university where he taught for forty years needed to be told about him suggests how much criticism has changed in the past thirty years.

Babbitt's genius was fundamentally homiletic. Below the homily lay dogma. He regarded the books he taught as sources of texts to expound. Naturally he was often accused of distorting the texts, and many of the accusations were justified. He could, for example, read Rousseau's celebrated "the man who thinks is a depraved animal" as if Rousseau were taking *depraved* in the exclusively moral sense and as if being a defective animal were exactly equivalent to being a defective human being. He was not given to preserving the context of what he quoted, and less disposed to select passages which revealed the intention of their author than those which supported or made clear the appositeness of his own doctrine.

Doctrine was what counted: his three realms of existence —the natural, the human, and the supernatural—provided the basis of an ethic. He could not use the supernatural, because religion escaped him except in so far as it affected conduct, but between the other two "planes" there was no question: there was law for man and law for thing, and it was the law for man—recognizing in man what was not animal or natural and could be hypostasized as an inner check or sense of decorum—which should prevail. And which, he thought, threatened not to prevail because of the corrupting influences, first, of Baconian positivism, and second, of Romanticism and Rousseau. Rousseau was the clearest and most present danger because of his eloquence, having invented nothing but set everything on fire. Romanticism had contaminated men's emotions and thus eventually their whole life. Babbitt was against it, he said, because it had not made men happy.

From these principles he derived his attitudes toward literature, politics, education, and, more generally, toward

life as he knew it. His severity toward modern literature
was absolute. Romanticism had pervaded everything—and
Naturalism was Romanticism on all fours; ours, he wrote,
was the fifth Romantic generation; all women, all children,
and most men were Romanticists. By his standards, much
nineteenth-century writing was unhealthy, and that of the
twentieth was even more so. Even those who tended to
agree with him were frightened by his disposition to pour
out the baby with the bath. One group of young poets and
critics challenged him in public print to name a single
modern poet of whose work he approved. Since, on the face
of it, most modern literature still derived—if generalized
terms ending in "-ism" have any application at all—from
Naturalism or Symbolism, he knew that he stood small
chance of satisfying his interrogators and declined the
gambit. In his published criticism, as a matter of record, he
had little to say about recent writing, although those who
knew him reported that he read his contemporaries exten-
sively. His books confined themselves mostly to explaining
his general attitude and promoting his general ideas.

The New Laokoön and Rousseau and Romanticism
remain as monumental reminders of the moment when
conservative criticism in France and America moved toward
"the liquidation of Romanticism." Masters of Modern French
Criticism, reacting against the "impressionism" of Jules
Lemaître and Anatole France and the "dilettantism" of the
Huneker-Spingarn-Mencken tradition in the United States,
revealed Babbitt's admiration for Sainte-Beuve, although he
deplored the latter's "Epicurean relaxation" and his "ency-
clopedic curiosity." Babbitt would have been happy had
Sainte-Beuve's gifts been combined with Emerson's devotion
to the life of the spirit. His preference among critics for one
as far out of sympathy with his contemporaries as was
Saint-Beuve is probably characteristic. Criticism, he argued,

must discriminate rigorously in contemporary writing to discover whatever good there is in it. "Discriminate" appears very frequently in Babbitt's prose. He did not disguise its implication of a willingness and even a predisposition to reject.

Much, if not most, that has happened in American criticism of the past thirty years could be adumbrated by a juxtaposition of Babbitt's favorite word with the one which plays a similar role in the work of his former pupil who has been called to the Irving Babbitt Chair. This does not mean that Harry Levin does not advocate discrimination, but the verb which is operative in his criticism, as "discriminate" is in Babbitt's, is "explicate." Behind the difference lies Babbitt's implicit assumption that literature is a static body containing the world's wisdom (and unwisdom) to be used by the individual as a guide for life, as contrasted with Levin's view of literature as an aspect of dynamic civilization —what he calls literature as institution. Whereas Babbitt was occupied with setting up danger signals, Levin is concerned with setting up points of reference, as his repetition of two other terms, "perspective" and "context," would suggest. His multifold allusiveness—leafing through one seventeen-page essay I have just counted seventy-three mentions of authors and titles—becomes a method of surrounding the subject of the moment with a multiplicity of vantage points and a way to coerce the reader with as many comparisons and contrasts, until the subject acquires a full set of meanings, and a freshness which comes from having been viewed from angles to which he has not become dulled through habituation.

Babbitt would doubtless condemn Levin's "curiosity"; books on Joyce, Marlowe, and Hamlet, long studies of Proust, Stendhal, Balzac, Flaubert, Poe, Hawthorne, and Melville, plus evidence of other critical activity which has taken him across a half-dozen literatures, suggest the kind of "inclusive-ness" of which his old teacher was exceedingly wary. One may doubt, however, that Babbitt would have gone on to add the epithet "Epicurean," since the pupil's intention is relentlessly, though not menacingly, elucidative.

Levin, like his master, is a semanticist, too aware of what words mean to use a term like "explication" loosely. His unorthodox use of it must be regarded as intentional, and as a sign of modesty. For *explication de texte,* as understood by those who practice it as a way of life, is a modestly pedagogical, not a critical, discipline. It consists of demon-strating in the fullest detail appropriate to the instance, using a fragment of text chosen *ad hoc,* that the established manuals are right in what they say about a given work of a given writer. Nothing more can come out of it than goes in. This discipline was installed in the French public schools by the Reform of 1902 as a means of curbing teachers whose classroom techniques consisted of imitating the dilettantish essays of Jules Lemaître or the oratorical dogmatism of Ferdinand Brunetière. Surely, a method like Levin's, which aspires to discover in a text precisely what has not been adequately remarked in it before, deserves a name more capable of defining the nature of his enterprise.

But terminology aside, the nature of the enterprise itself is what marks the distance criticism has traversed since the heyday of Babbitt and his New Humanism. What has happened in the interim is the kind of history which, because it was once so familiar, has become inordinately easy to forget.

The first consequence of Babbitt's writing about educa-tion was a sort of polarization. Almost singlehanded he had created the dichotomy of criticism versus "scholarship"—as if scholars could not be critical or critics scholarly. He had alienated the philologists by his assertion, in *Literature and the American College,* that a firm grounding in the classics was more desirable equipment for a teacher of literature than experience with the European Middle Ages, and the historians of literature by identifying their pursuit of the circumstantial context with naturalistic positivism, which he held to imply the neglect of "standards." He had also expressed strong doubts about the Ph.D., which he did not hold himself, and about the practicability and wisdom of teaching "creative" writing in the classroom. All these endeavors seemed to him to encourage the dilettantish attitude which, to put it more mildly than he ever did, he condemned.

Subsequent repolarizations were various. Babbitt's followers were largely in the universities, whereas critics and writers operating in the world outside tended to line up very solidly against him. He had rejected too much. A book like Edmund Wilson's *Axel's Castle* acquired a significance present-day readers hardly imagine from constituting, as it did at the beginning of the thirties, an implicit denial of the New Humanist stand that recent Symbolism was nothing if not deliquescent. And critics like Malcolm Cowley had no trouble showing that the literature of the decade just ended had been serious in a way Babbitt had not suspected. Beside such men, though on different grounds, the critics of the intellectual Left naturally took their stand as the Proletarian Decade got under way: they had no more patience left than did George Santayana for what they called middle-class gentility. But while as a movement the New Humanism rapidly played out after Babbitt's death, when the already conservative *Bookman* gave way to the reactionary *American Review,* criticism proceeded to establish itself firmly in the universities.

At Columbia the group which clustered about Mark Van Doren effected a coup of which Babbitt might well have

approved when they took the freshman literature course out
of the hands of the English department, substituted a series
of complete texts (from Homer to Goethe) for the snippets
in the anthologies which had previously made up the pro-
gram, and ruled that the history of literature was of little
relevance to the kind of reading job they wanted their
students to undertake. Weak in theory where their predecessors at Chicago had been strong, but able to staff the
course with teachers like Van Doren, Weaver, Trilling,
Barzun, and Edman, and in a position to recruit men like
F. M. Dupee and Richard Chase, they had superior man-
power, and the success of their attempt to establish a critical
dialogue between teacher and student as the central teaching
method started a landslide. "Humanities" courses, "Great
Books," and "World Literature" rapidly moved in, all about
the country.

Almost simultaneously, English departments were sub-
jected to new pressures, often generated from within. The
old "Fugitives" from Vanderbilt, like Ransom, Warren, and
Tate, joined by Cleanth Brooks and several of the agrarians
of *I'll Take My Stand,* were talking of the poem-as-ontology,
of "autotelic" and organic literature, of new readings of old
poems—studying "structure and texture" and the "tensions"
within the text. They published interesting criticism in the
Southern Review and subsequently in the *Kenyon.* In their
first careless rapture they were anti-historical, and before
they finished they had forced *P.M.L.A.,* once a bastion of
historical scholarship, to change the definition of its function
and admit them to its pages. Enlightened textbooks edited
by Brooks and Warren took the new attitude into the colleges
and even the secondary schools: at this writing, the National
Advanced Placement examination, by which youngsters
show that they have anticipated a year of college English
while still in high school, requires no historical information—

and I have examined graduate students at the Doctor's oral who clearly regarded questions involving dates as uncouth if not downright obscene.

A second edition of *Understanding Poetry* by Brooks and Warren contained a new "Letter to the Teacher" warning against the excess of abandoning history entirely. Too late: second editions do not have the impact of first editions, and the tendency remains, in spite of efforts of people like Ransom to cool the ardor of the extreme enthusiasts. Properly applied, their method was linguistic—philology applied to the study of form—and required a training which not all of its adherents possessed; some of their errors are now embalmed in the folklore of criticism. But learned Europeans like Leo Spitzer, Erich Auerbach, and Helmuth Hatzfeld, and the refugees from Russian and Czech formalism, joined the periphery of the group and lent it a compensating authority.

Too much has been alleged about the political orientation of the New Criticism. Doubtless one did not have to take a political stand in order to practice it; doubtless these critics could study politically repellent poets (e.g. Pound) without explicitly rejecting the ideas of their subjects; doubtless when they turned to the study of prose they were free to avert their faces from the politically hot fiction of the moment and gorge themselves on the later novels of Henry James. Given the political climate of the United States after World War II, the attractiveness of a critical practice which did not oblige the critic to expose himself should not be underestimated: it may even have facilitated the survival of criticism. But the signal fact is that criticism had, as never before, become cloistered.

It would be idle to claim, of course, that in previous generations criticism had not been a professorial function: for every Saintsbury there have always been a dozen Arnolds,

Sainte-Beuves, and Taines. But the earlier critics, while teaching in their universities, had lived a double life, regularly addressing a public on the outside. In the American thirties, not only critics but criticism moved into the academy: critical method and pedagogical method were in a way to becoming identical. More and more, criticism was written by academics for an academic audience. The "autotelic" critic could not expect to find space even in magazines addressed to a restricted cultivated public. Rarely did a neocritical study make the pages of such generally academic quarterlies as the *Yale Review*. Criticism became a recognized academic discipline, but in the process its practitioners were reduced to taking in each other's washing.

New Criticism died hard but—except as a classroom method—die it did. By the time René Wellek and Austin Warren published their *Theory of Literature*, which was intended as an "organon of method" as seen from the neocritical vantage, its authors found themselves pushing violently on an already open door; except for a few Europeans who had joined American faculties but lately, the most the old-fashioned historians were asking was that theirs be considered a viable discipline *also*, and when resistance ceases such movements lose their impetus. (The battle of the New Criticism now survives, curiously, only among the members of the Sorbonne, one of whom, René Jasinski, in an introduction to a book on Racine, has just performed the curious ritual of kicking a horse fifteen years dead.) The great question thereafter was what would develop next. Now that it was so securely in, how would criticism contrive to move out of the universities again?

Like the New Humanism, the New Criticism had been a regional phenomenon, but one of a different region, flowering principally at a distance from the metropolitan areas and away from the Atlantic Coast as its predecessor had thriven best along the seaboard. With the possible exception of Yale, it had never penetrated deeply, so long as its form remained pure, into the large eastern or far-western institutions. But while it occupied the heartland, as it unquestionably did, New Criticism resolutely averted its eyes from the local scene. Studies proliferated on James and Melville, Emily Dickinson and Katherine Anne Porter; Hemingway, Faulkner, and Fitzgerald came in for a large share of attention; so did a few recent poets like Wallace Stevens. But by and large, writers who had to report the experience of living in the environment they were all living in were largely neglected, and this is almost as true of the poets as of the novelists.

It is true that the kind of highly organic literature their method worked best on had been written in other times and in other places, and that in a sense these critics were mildly alienated by a concept of their own function which tended to turn them away from the here and now. But one may suspect that this consideration is minor as compared with another: that criticism as an *academic* practice inherently deflects the attention from the current. The study of the teacher, which the academy is supposed to, and often does, provide leisure to pursue, rightfully should enrich teaching: it will thus tend to bear upon what he is teaching or planning to teach—and what he plans to teach is not what is being written at the moment. In fact, time devoted to current literary production is so likely to be time wasted, since one cannot know whether the written work justifies the expenditure of effort until too late, that the prudential advantage of studying what may often have been already abundantly studied, but is recognized as fully worthy of study, is mountainous.

One of the effects of all this is a strange compartmentalization of literary activities, which is best illustrated by a concrete example. (Fortunately the men concerned are my friends and will not take amiss their being cited in this context.) John Hawkes is a respected young novelist whose work has begun to attract serious attention; Edwin Honig is a poet whose work also commands respect. The two taught together in one New England university, and moved at the same time to another where again they teach in the same department. Their relations have been warmly friendly for years. Yet, although each combines critical writing with his imaginative work, so far as I know and up to this writing,* neither man has at any point undertaken a critical discussion of the writing of the other! I find myself fully persuaded that they live in the only not-underdeveloped country under heaven where such a situation could exist, but it is true that in America such a divorce between critical and "creative" functioning is common; witness the case of the late James Agee, whose friends had been familiar with his work for years but "discovered" him only when he was dead.

A graver consequence is that our criticism fails to perform a service which is one of the most important it could hope to furnish and perhaps the only one which fully justifies the continued existence of critics as a genus: it does little if anything to maintain and develop an appropriate climate in which literature as a whole—Harry Levin's "institution"— can prosper healthily. Few of us would be naïve enough to believe, today, that criticism affects other writing directly or that it should do so; many of us do not even believe that the *Edinburgh Review* killed John Keats. But it does seem reasonable to suppose that an active criticism, concerned

---

*This was true when I wrote it, but I now learn that Hawkes has since then published in *Voices* (January-April, 1961) a very brief piece on Honig's work, "The Voice of Edwin Honig." In view of the brevity of his comment and the restricted circulation of the periodical my remark seems to me *almost* as true as it ever was and accordingly I have let it stand.

with the writing of its contemporaries, does and should stir
a continuum of interest by its continual inquiry into meaning,
relevance, and value, and thus continually revitalize a public.

The notion is abroad that such a public does not exist—
and the notion turns an antlered dilemma into a paradox.
Here we are in 1961, after nearly thirty years of teaching
our young to read literature in a way which, if it is assumed
to do anything at all, is supposed to sensitize them to literature and open for them the road to literary pleasure. Our
schools and colleges have been increasingly populated and
now overflow; every June our campuses throng with eager
young graduates who must, if they do not go out to constitute
a public, immediately slough off the literary education for
which we have claimed so much. In all this teeming horde
there must be those few thousand who later make up the
elite which in any country reads books thoughtfully, for
nourishment and delight. Since criticism has been installed
within the academy it has had their ears. One has to conclude
that they have not liked the sound. Or that, once outside
the walls, they rapidly discover that what they have been
hearing, for a time varying from one semester to four years,
is not particularly relevant to the experience on which they
have embarked.

The blame and shame need not be laid exclusively at
the door of the New Critics, however influential they may
have been. We have also had with us the New York
Ideologists, whose favorite and perhaps characteristic vehicle
was long the *Partisan Review*. As opposed to the others,
they had at least a sense of involvement in the country which
produced the literature, even when they turned out not to
know enough about it. They too, in spite of themselves in
some cases, have been academics. Even Alfred Kazin, the
latest to protest against academic ways in criticism (see
Commentary for November, 1960), and Leslie Fiedler,

whose attempts to bring Marx, Jung, Pavlov, Freud, and
Kinsey to bear at once on American writing have brought
him to the conclusion that our novel does not deal adequately
with couples who are on their way to bed, are essentially
professors and dependent upon the hospitable shelter of
academic walls, trapped there perhaps but there none the
less. These critics, too, have had and still have the golden
opportunity to train and form a public.

Even those who live there admit that New York has
advantages, some of which are exclusively its own—very little
dramatic criticism, for example, can be expected to come
from outside the Five Boroughs. The critic who lives there
is within telephone call of his fellows, and of publishers
and of book clubs. But to recommend life in New York, as
Dwight Macdonald does in his article on James Gould
Cozzens, as a sort of prophylaxis against crabbedness and
eccentricity would seem to be the act of an optimist. The
concentricity and sunny urbanity of the *New Yorker*, a
magazine in which Macdonald sometimes writes, do not
strike everyone as convincingly genuine. And the price one
pays, or which in a number of conspicuous cases has been
exacted, of losing perspective upon the rest of the country,
is exorbitant.

For American liberals, New York was the center of the
Great Letdown of 1939, which did so much to alienate the
liberal mind and disorient liberal thought. The damage
wrought by the discovery that the Russians were cynically
selling out the Spanish republicans, and later that Stalin
was capable of the nonaggression agreement with Hitler,
left the words "liberal" and "intellectual" enshrined as
honorific, but the pinnacle of faith which had once given
the political idealist his special perspective upon America,
and hence his feeling of fixed relationship with the rest
of the country, rapidly crumbled. The feeling, nurtured by

the mass-information magazines and very largely justified by the happenings of the McCarthy years, that the liberal has no appointed place, has come to color the thought even of men who were not born soon enough to remember the original catastrophe. They feel cut off: witness their conviction, transparent both in their styles and in what they say, that their fate is to write for radically restricted audiences.

While it is true that the New York critics have escaped the inhibitions of the New Criticism, their home is also the home of what someone has called a "low voltage" *Angst*. The presence of a large—and valuable—concentration of ex-European intellectuals, more aware than any American can be of the uncertainties and horrors of the recent past, doubtless intensifies it by making the city the point from which the horrors of the future look most unavoidable. I have no desire to decry, or deprive myself of the pleasures and benefits of reading, the criticism of men like Lionel Trilling, Philip Rahv, Richard Chase, Fred Dupee, and various others, but the chances of their ever animating the public which our criticism should animate seem to me relatively feeble.

Let whatever will be said about Irving Babbitt, including much that will undoubtedly be unfavorable and most likely true, no one will take the stand that he was out of touch with his country. Living in what, for his time, came nearest to being an ivory tower, he was still mightily concerned with the contemporary United States. A British observer, Marcus Cunliffe, has pointed out that what David Riesman and his associates now claim to be happening to this country is what, thirty years ago, Babbitt was afraid might happen. Babbitt's lifelong attempt to trace the historical development of the ideas and attitudes he disliked strikes us today as simplistic and "unscholarly" precisely because he was less intent upon what had happened in the past than upon what was threatening to happen in the very imminent future. What he said about Rousseau was monstrously unfair to Rousseau, but what he said about life in the United States had at least the virtue of being said about something he felt very much a part of, so much a part that he was unfair to Rousseau. He hated Rousseau because he saw a filiation between Rousseau and Henry Ford, between Rousseau and the cult of bigness, between Rousseau and a willingness to substitute quantity for quality. His language should not mislead us at this point: he meant by commercial vulgarity what we mean by the neon wilderness; what he pictured as humanitarianism is what Peter De Vries is getting at in the Community Church whose pastor-manager is the Reverend Mr. Mackerel and which includes everything, even a "worship area." Babbitt did not feel cut off, either by the nature of the writing he criticized or by the unpopularity of his position, from the audience on which he intended to exercise an influence.

The inauguration of the first Irving Babbitt Professor consecrates a development which has been three decades in process, for in it erudition is placed in the service of criticism, and criticism—as it was not in Babbitt's time—is fully accepted as a mode of teaching. But by the nature of university chairs the influence of the incumbent threatens to be left behind when his disciples leave the halls of learning. If what our writing tells us about life in America is true, the undergraduate years are the individual's first experience in moving from one area of culture to another. At graduation he stands likely to undergo the second, when he moves not homeward to the first familiar area but away toward some employment which promises to put him in a third, and again unfamiliar one. Whether at that point he becomes a member of the elite or leaves his education behind and settles into an other-directed *Lumpen-bourgeoisie* is an open question.

For the purpose of inculcating durable cultural interests it may not be enough to give him even the finest instruction in literature as an art, broadly conceived, just as it has not been enough in recent years to give him instruction in literature as an art, narrowly conceived.

Now that Babbitt's battle to get criticism into the university has been won, the next necessary step may well be to get it out again—or at least to make sure that its public influence gets exercised upon individuals who are beyond the university age. To achieve this last, what our critics say, while continuing to be relevant to what is read in college, will have to be relevant to life as it is lived after graduation.

10

Images and Myths

QUITE APART from any consideration of his merits as a social scientist, David Riesman should get credit for being one of the noteworthy poets of the last decade. Or, if not exactly for being a poet, then for being something more or less similar, the creator of an image. I mean image not in the public relations sense, which is little more than something designed to keep the public from getting an adequate view of some reality, but in the sense of something to which men's imaginations can attach themselves until it becomes part of what they live by. This is image in a meaning which relates it to myth: we accept it implicitly and it determines our attitudes and actions. Yeats meant very much the same thing by his "powerful emblem."

Giving Riesman this credit is something I would greatly have liked to be the first to do, but unfortunately Norman Mailer, if no one else, has done it ahead of me. I do not care much for *Advertisements for Myself,* even though we all recognize the existence of some force or other in the current ethos which makes it necessary for writers of any stature above the minimum to undress themselves, morally, in public; Mailer manages to jockey his reader into the position of a voyeur, and the reader naturally feels some resentment. But his perception that Riesman is an image-making artist is entirely right and may not be rejected.

Riesman's image of the "other-directed" American, shaping his life to win the approval of his neighbors and thus tending to become as much like them as possible, has behind it the authority of a social scientist, but it has reached out to, and caught the imagination of, a public which until quite recently the product of the social sciences rarely touched at all. When its author let *The Lonely Crowd* go into an edition for lay consumption, in a form which relieved the ordinary run of readers of the burden of wading through all the supporting data, he exposed himself to the kind of understanding that is as much as the mass audience is able to give, a kind of crude and general comprehension, a grasping at a central idea at the expense of all the qualifying considerations. What most of us kept from reading *The Lonely Crowd* was the image of an American always identical with himself and essentially featureless, uncompetitive and hypersensitive to the opinions of his peers, who for various reasons, which we could not state but which were "scientific," was on the way to becoming the only American who could possibly be; the American character either was changing or had changed. This image is the first seriously to challenge the image of the American seen as a victim of chronic displacement which has been dominant in so much of our literature.

Riesman's "other-directed" American has not caught on in literature, of course, in the way the image of the American as D.P. caught on. If I am right, the typical hero dominating the writing of the years when the data for *The Lonely Crowd* were being collected is of a quite different sort. Since the book was first published in 1949, the observations which support it must come from about the same period as those which provide the stuff of such books as *The Catcher in the Rye*, *The Invisible Man*, and *The Adventures of Augie March*, novels with heroes who are displaced and on the

move, who have no door where they can enter; the most
noteworthy difference between such characters and earlier
samples of displacement is that at least two of the three
have increasing difficulty coping with life at all, because
too much happens to them too fast. Holden Caulfield ends
up in a sanitarium; Ellison's fugitive hero is last seen
cowering in a coalbin. Surely their troubles are not those
of a type who keeps his social "radar" turned outward. And
Augie March is hardly disposed to conform beyond the
point necessary to keep him out of jail. These three novels,
which are certainly among the most memorable of their
decade, stand witness to a feeling of life in America very
different from the one which Riesman brought forward.

One might have expected that "other-directed" heroes
would begin to appear in the novel after *The Lonely Crowd*
had gone into paperback, but the flurry of effort, in the
early fifties, to put gray flannel into fiction was brief and
its product lacked distinction. What happened was that
by 1954 the "other-directed" had begun feeding the mills
of satire. Max Shulman worked over the station-wagon
matriarchy in *Rally Round the Flag, Boys!* And Peter
De Vries, moving into the area as though he owned it, has
operated happily there ever since. Unless Riesman's American turns out to be the exception which finally proved the
rule, present chances of his eventually winning a place in
our writing look thin: once a hero type has won the
attention of the satirists, its later appearance in straight
literature is highly unlikely.

Its failure to take a place in literature may help define
the nature of the "other-directed" image, but—let this be
emphasized—does not indicate a lack of emblematic power.
The strength of Riesman's creation is that it fills a very real
need, at least for readers of a certain experience of American
life, by which I mean those of Riesman's own generation. We

emerged from the colleges into the Great Depression. There was very little we could do for ourselves; everything was out of our hands; economic Forces were at work; everything that happened was inevitable. Shortly thereafter we perceived that another set of Forces were at work, and now it was war in Europe that was inevitable and again there was nothing we could do about it. The one hope, for many, was that still different Forces would bring out of the war a revolution which would make things better. Then war came, and we learned that by the laws which govern such things the United States would eventually be involved. We did get involved, and for a few more years we did not what we wanted but what circumstances beyond our control made us do. For fifteen years of his life the American of the particular age in question thought of himself as a creature driven by one kind of fate or another. Then came peace, and when we looked around to see what was driving us now, nothing was in sight.

Fifteen years is a long enough time for habits to become firmly set. It was confusing, in the years between 1945 and 1950, to be on the loose in a world which was mostly welter but which seemed to be pushing us in no special direction. Not to think of ourselves as fated characters was almost the equivalent of not thinking of ourselves at all. It was in this vacuum that David Riesman loosed the notion of the "other-directed" character, and once more we could imagine ourselves as being in the grip of Forces. And as it turned out, the years when the general reading public became aware of *The Lonely Crowd* were also the years when we were most aware of Senator McCarthy, who may have accomplished nothing else but who surely convinced his countrymen of the great prudential value of inconspicuousness and protective coloring. Riesman's image of the American did not need to find its way into imaginative literature in order

to acquire power; it had the power all the time, the power
of any image or any myth which helps us make sense of
a predicament which is ours and which, without the aid of
the image, seems meaningless.

Consequently it would appear that the American imagination is capable of entertaining two images of the American
at the same time, and that these two contradict each other.
It is true that contradiction has never bothered the best of us
very deeply: money is filthy lucre yet good to have, etc. But
in the present case the contradiction is based on verifiable
facts. Surely an impressive cultural variety must have existed
in the country at one point or the Great Topos of displace-
ment-in-diversity would not have achieved the dimensions it
clearly has achieved. Just as surely, a considerable cultural
uniformity must exist or Riesman's image would not have
prospered, but even the appearance of this new image has
not silenced the testimony to cultural diversity. We never
get very far from a paradox which remains the same in
essence although it may be stated in a number of different
ways. Sociology says that the national character is being
transformed; literature is almost unaware of any such change.
The country is menaced by a creeping conformity, yet is
also threatened by the disaffection of nobody knows how
many—though surely too many—young and creative people.
Men like President Conant are concerned by the divisiveness
of our institutions; men like John Dos Passos, to judge by
Midcentury, are eaten by fear of our growing to be so alike
we cannot be told apart. There is evidence that Americans
feel at home nowhere in their country; there is other evidence
that nowhere they go can they avoid seeing what they have
always seen and doing what they have always done. One
visits Oxford, Mississippi, and finds a town little different
from many others, but one gets from the reading about
Faulkner's Jefferson the conviction that nowhere else could

the feel and quality of life be quite the same. The paradox is both omnipresent and multiform.

It was prominently present at the presidential inauguration of 1961 when, after four clergymen had prayed, Marian Anderson had sung the national anthem, and John F. Kennedy had dedicated himself to his job, Robert Frost stood up to read his poem. The prayers, the singing, and the dedication had been the standard parts of our quadrennial tribal gesture of appeal to what we hold to be self-evident; they were, so to speak, undenominational and uncontroversial, acceptable to all. What should not escape our attention is that the poet was on the platform for the same purpose, and under the same auspices, as the other participants. The nature of the paradox comes out into the light when we remember that the poet was Robert Frost.

Frost would be our laureate if we could have a laureate. He is the one poet most literate Americans have heard of who is also admired by those who actually read poetry, the only one recognized as good for children who does not insult the intelligence of adults. He stands for poetry on the national level.

And yet among all the poets of the land, this same Robert Frost stands out for having exploited to the limit the cultural differences within the country. Without ceasing to incarnate the Poet for the country at large, he is most specifically the laureate of the granite ridges and second-growth hardwoods of a particular region. For all the talk about universal symbols in his work and about his making New Hampshire a microcosm, this Californian born who wrote his first poems in England represents the persistent belief that only in a special landscape does one see life steadily and see it whole—and speak well of it if somewhat laconically also. The wall that something there is that doesn't love runs the line between two upland New England farms, and, to most of Frost's faithful readers, the poem it appears in is not a statement about the general problem of men's living side by side with other men. In short, the poet— himself a symbol—who lent his presence to the ceremonial of our country-wide togetherness was the one who has testified, all his life long, that in the matters that count most we are not together. You *can* go home again, runs the lesson of his poetry, but you had better stay there once you go because you won't be completely yourself anywhere else. In his way Frost has paid as much tribute as anyone to the Great Topos of American displacement.

That he stood there in Washington, half-blinded by the harsh January sun, to fumble his way through the good lines about how the land was ours before we were the land's, reveals the power of the nationally accepted idea that certain commodities are good for us all. Frost's poetry is good for us. It is also good for us to fill our homes with reproductions which make the original paintings look muddy and with high-fidelity recordings which are played in more comfort, and with less extraneous noise, than could be possible in any concert hall, just as it is good for us to fill our shelves with expert and competently written books on every important subject. These are the things of the spirit, available to all: you can be sure of getting unexceptionable ones, chosen by Jacques Barzun and others whose taste is guaranteed never to let you look bad, by filling out a coupon and sending in a small check monthly. These things are good; we want them for our children and the PTA wants them in our schools. The call of PTA-culture was what brought Frost to Washington, the call of a cultural phenomenon which David Riesman has taught us to see as a manifestation of "other-directedness."

Frost answered the call—but does this mean the triumph of uniformity over diversity? Or is there some possibility that the ideal of a culturally diverse country has emerged from partial eclipse and may yet play a part in shaping the country's ends? I am encouraged to think so by a reading of the satirists, like Max Shulman and Peter De Vries, who have taken the "other-directed" to be their special targets. Their formula is classically simple: it consists of transplanting a group of other-directed urbanites from New York to the Connecticut countryside, within commuting distance of the big city yet far enough from it so that the local tone is not metropolitan but hardshell Yankee. Both writers state the situation in terms not only that the sociologists would understand but also that they have actually used. And the story rises out of the inherent frictions. Shulman's Harry Bannerman has a wife so taken up with the doings of the little community—Town Meeting, Garbage Disposal, and, yes, PTA—that out of sheer frustration he becomes an unwilling, and not particularly convincing, adulterer. De Vries' Reverend Andrew Mackerel, pastor of the "People's Liberal" Church in a similar community on Long Island Sound, teaches a religion that can be understood only in the light of books like Will Herberg's *Protestant, Catholic, Jew;* his troubles arise when he discovers that a fair share of his parishioners are not deeply enthusiastic about a church which is a combination of psychiatric clinic, bowling alley, and babysitting service and would instinctively prefer what appealed to their "inner-directed" Yankee forebears.

It is not entirely fair to Lionel Trilling's highly serious novel to point out that Shulman's and De Vries' formula is also the formula of *The Middle of the Journey*, since Trilling's intention reaches well beyond the exploitation of a comic predicament. But it must be clear that no great change in the angle of vision would have been needed to bring out the latent comic possibilities of the uneasy juxtaposition of the two cultural groups which his hero, Laskell, fails to recognize. A similar shift, entailing, as in Trilling's case also, a transfer of social loyalties, could have made a comedy out of Cozzens' *By Love Possessed*. The comic potential of *The Great Gatsby*, even though this novel antedates Riesman's formulation by so many years, reveals certain similarities.

There may not be quite so much to say for current satire as I think there is: admittedly it lacks bite and could stand a stronger admixture of acid in the formula. And in any event this is not the place to go into my admiration for the work of Peter De Vries. But whatever the quality of such writing, and whether or not it turns out to constitute a significant revival of the comic novel as I think it does, the fact that it exists and is widely read (by readers who must include no few of the character type De Vries finds so amusing) is extremely relevant to the present topic: what such satirists are saying is that when types like Andrew Mackerel and Harry Bannerman find their way into literature, they do so as displaced persons faced by the necessity to adjust to an alien cultural environment. In other words, "other-directed" man takes his place among the many who cluster about the Great Topos.

The only other literary area where one can find Riesman's image being put to work is the one patrolled by the Beats. To them, since they need footballs, it is useful, but the use they make of it twists the image considerably. They hate the outward signs of uniformity, the nasty little houses all alike wherein nasty little people lead lives which are alike and nasty also. And so forth along the familiar line. But the houses and the rest are not, for the convinced Beat, connected with the notion of tranquil and comfortable existence. They are a part of living in "the rat race"—and it is good to get away from them as it is good to get away from the rest of a civilization which, always according to the Beats, always overemphasizes, rather than de-emphasizes, competition. Possibly what is important here is not that the image as elaborated by Riesman has been warped, but that it is an image in conflict with others. The existence of the conflict tells its own story.

All this begins to suggest that there was nothing particularly incongruous in the presence of Robert Frost on the platform in Washington, and that the cultural situation in the United States at this moment is infinitely more complex than a reading of books like *The Lonely Crowd* has led us to think. Undoubtedly the images, myths, and *topoi* which a civilization breeds correspond to social realities, past and present; undoubtedly the same imaginative phenomena in their turn react upon the realm of social "fact" and help to form the realities which at any moment are in the process of succeeding those with which we have grown familiar. Views of the future, invariably hedged by qualifiers like "if conditions, including the economic ones, continue the same," are in turn conditioned by the fact that staying the same is the one thing such conditions do not do. There is no final solution, in other words, to the paradoxes, real or apparent, which result from an examination of the subject. All that can be said with any confidence at all is that any account of American writing which does not take the question of cultural differences into account is doomed to be something less than entirely complete.

Index